WE ARE ONE

UNLOCKING GENERATIONAL UNITY AND THE FUTURE OF YOUR CHURCH

K.W. NEWSOME

We Are One
Unlocking Generational Unity and
the Future of Your Church
by
K.W. Newsome

ISBN-10: 0-9989596-0-X
ISBN-13: 978-0-9989596-0-3

© 2017 Keven Newsome
Cover Art © 2017 Newsome Creative
All Rights Reserved

www.KevenNewsome.com

A
PRESS EPIC
Publication

Scripture quotations taken from the New American
Standard Bible® (NASB),
Copyright © 1960, 1962, 1963, 1968, 1971, 1972, 1973,
1975, 1977, 1995 by The Lockman Foundation
Used by permission. www.Lockman.org

TABLE OF CONTENTS

The Generational Imperative 1

Dividing the Generations 8

The Silent Generation 16

The Baby Boomers 27

Generation X 36

Millennials 46

The iGeneration 56

Generational Relationships 65

Generation Cycles 81

The Cycle of the Church 94

Ministry Strategies 110

Now What? 125

Bibliography 131

DEDICATION/ACKNOWLEDGMENTS

This book represents three years' worth of slow work. It started as a simple discipleship study, but thanks to the encouragement of church members and friends it has finally become something people can hold in their hands. It's to those people I want to dedicate this book. Without their constant prodding, it almost certainly wouldn't have happened. I can't thank all of you personally, so if you're one of those who urged me to complete this project…thank you.

However, there are some specific people I'd like to acknowledge.

As always, I want to thank my lovely wife, DeAnna, who is a constant source of encouragement and my biggest cheerleader.

To Zach, Becky, and Susan: thank you for the read-throughs and editing help.

To Chris, Bobby, Craigan, Scott, and Will: thank you for the support you've shown during my difficult times of ministry.

CHAPTER 1

THE GENERATIONAL IMPERATIVE

"For even as the body is one and yet has many members, and all the members of the body, though they are many, are one body, so also is Christ." 1 Corinthians 12:12

We're living in a post-modern, post-Christian[1] society in which the church establishment is struggling to find ways to reconnect with culture and to reconnect with the next generation, a generation that is meant to take over the church when current church leaders are gone. In this struggle, churches are becoming increasingly aware that lines of division have been drawn between the generations. Seldom do you now see a church with a healthy mix of all age groups. This is a problem. Older generations of the church are beginning to feel the urgency to train their replacements and to leave the

---

[1] Post-Christian simply means that Christianity is no longer the default lens through which our society operates.

church in trusted hands, yet there are few hands to be found willing to take on the task. These churches are looking around and wondering where all the young families are and what they can do to bring them back.

Allow me to give you the short answer to the question of where they are. The ones that are church goers are mostly going to churches populated by people of their own age groups, and the older traditional church doesn't appeal to them any longer.

Sure, the situation is far more complex than that simple statement. There is an entire post-Christian culture that's often more appealing to younger generations than establishment religion. This is not meant to be a book on how to win back these generations from culture, but a book to understand the religious expectations of ALL generations so that churches can adjust their thinking to be more generationally inclusive.

When it comes to what many would consider healthy churches in America, a two church type structure seems to have developed. There are the "traditional" models, more attractive to older generations, and the "modern" models, more attractive to younger generations. Traditional churches struggle to be relevant and attract younger people. Modern churches seem to have given up on traditionalism all-together, and therefore are perceived as not friendly to senior adults.

God did not mean for the church to be divided along age lines. He meant for the church to be united in service to him. Paul, in his letter to Titus, gives us the best picture of what God means for the church to look like generationally.

> *"Older men are to be temperate, dignified, sensible, sound in faith, in love, in perseverance. Older women likewise are to be reverent in their behavior, not malicious gossips nor enslaved to much wine, teaching what is good, so that they may encourage the young women to love their husbands, to love their children, to be sensible, pure, workers at home, kind, being subject to their own husbands, so that the word of God will not be dishonored. Likewise, urge the young men to be sensible; in all things show yourself to be an example of good deeds, with purity in doctrine, dignified, sound in speech which is beyond reproach, so that the opponent will be put to shame, having nothing bad to say about us." Titus 2:2–8*

We are meant to work together, not fight. And I think deep down we all want to stop the fighting, we want to be unified, we want to worship together…if we can all just get on the same page.

The world changed in the past fifty years. It has changed more in these past fifty years than perhaps at any point in history. The older generations have struggled to keep up, and the younger generations are running ahead almost recklessly. So a rift began that took root in the 1980s and began to pull the church apart in the 1990s.

Now in the late-2010s, it is more apparent than ever that our churches are divided and becoming more so almost daily. This dichotomy in church attendance can be boiled down to something relatively simple: older generations and younger generations don't understand each other and don't know how to work with each other. The church that figures this out and can become united generationally will be a growing, exciting, and dynamic church prepared to move forward in our culture and in the future of serving God.

The church that figures this out and can become united generationally will be a growing, exciting, and dynamic church...

I became interested in studying how the generations affected the church a few years ago when I became the thirty-something pastor of an aging congregation. They thought my presence would help bring younger families back to the church, but what they couldn't understand was that the issue wasn't with the leadership; it was with the deeper attitude of that older generation. They expected the younger generations to conform to their way of doing things, and at the same time, the younger generations felt the older methods were outdated. Until that deeper conflict could be resolved, they would always struggle to be relevant and to be united across age demographics.

This study was meant to help that church and other churches, both young and old, learn what it means to be united again. It is meant to be educational, so that every generation will not only understand the way the other generations think, but also have the tools and the knowledge necessary to react accordingly in order to build unity rather than foster division. It's also important to note that this study is ministerial for the purpose of helping churches. It is not a sociological study or sociologically perfect, though I have tried to include as much background and supporting data as was feasible.

Every church is different. Every region is different. Every community is different. Every family is different. And every person is different. This study is not meant to be one-size-fits-all for every situation. Rather, this study focuses on the general overall characteristics of the generations as wholes and as observed throughout our nation. It may not apply to every individual within the generation, every family, or every community…you get the idea. Characteristics may vary by region, upbringing, and experiences. If some of these things do not apply to you, do not take it personally. This is merely based on a generalization of your entire generation; from Maine to California, from Wisconsin to Mississippi, young and poor, educated and uneducated, churched and unchurched.

This study should also be used as a ministry tool to

help develop effective strategies to minister to people of all age groups and to minimize neglect. Through this, the leadership of a church can build effective church change in an appropriate way that will be supported by church members of all ages. Also, this study can be used to formulate effective church outreach to the demographics of their ministry circles.

Sounds too good to be true? Maybe it is, but at least this is a good place to start. If the generations can't begin to understand each other, we'll never begin to work together. How well this will help your church depends on how much of it is accepted and what the people genuinely want to do with this information. Every church is different, but the churches that figure out this generational dilemma and choose to do what is necessary to be united again will be the ones that survive.

REFLECTION QUESTIONS

1. Why is generational unity important in your church context?

2. What issues have hindered this unity?

3. What are some things that make your context unique in the world?

CHAPTER 2

DIVIDING THE GENERATIONS

"Great is the Lord, and highly to be praised, and His greatness is unsearchable. One generation shall praise Your works to another."
Psalm 145:3-4

My parents are Baby Boomers. My children are iGeneration. I was born within five years of the division between Generation X and Millennials. So what am I? Am I a Gen X or a Millennial?

The divisions between the generations can be subjective. In fact, many experts place the generational divides differently amongst each other and are not even close to a consensus. They look for markers in society and culture, historical events, population trends, and other division lines to which they can easily point. Some use a baseline year range of around fifteen years to determine generations, but even this division rule almost always relies on some major event or defining moment in history to help define that generation. (More on these defining

Dividing the Generations | 9

generational moments will be discussed in the chapter on Generation Cycles.)

So you can see, nailing down exactly where one generation ends and another begins is not an accurate science. There can be a two to five-year discrepancy about where these divisions occur. The dividing lines I have chosen for this study were determined by averaging the generational division lines from several different sources.[2] That means there can be a window of up to five years on either side of the division mark, where someone born on one side of the break might act and identify with the other side of the break. Lancaster and Stillman call those born in these break windows "cuspers," implying they are born in one generation but on the cusp of another.[3] However, I find the term lacking, still emphasizing a definitive break in the generational gap and not recognizing that those in the break are in a gray area likely to take on characteristics of both generations. I prefer to call these people break babies, implying they are in a window, or spectrum, of the

---

[2] George Barna, *Baby Busters: The Disillusioned Generation* (Chicago: Northfield Publishing, 1994), 14-15; William Strauss and Neil Howe, *The Fourth Turning: An American Prophecy* (New York: Broadway Books, 1998), 59; Thom S. Rainer and Jess W. Rainer, *The Millennials: Connecting to America's Largest Generation* (Nashville, Tenn: B&H Pub. Group, 2011), 2; "Generation," Wikipedia, the Free Encyclopedia, https://en.wikipedia.org/wiki/Generation (accessed April 13, 2016).

[3] Lynne C. Lancaster and David Stillman, *When Generations Collide: Who They Are, Why They Clash, How to Solve the Generational Puzzle at Work* (New York: HarperCollins, 2002), 36-41.

generational transition.

I am a break baby, which is why it is difficult to determine the generation with which I best identify.

Someone born in the break, but closer to the older generation side, may have children firmly in a generation two down from their own "calendar" generation. A generation gap is present, meaning there is an entire generational identity separating the parents and the children.

Generational identity gaps are largely unnatural. The natural order is that one generation begets the next. So to prevent the generation gap, parents born in a break may subconsciously shift to identifying with the younger generation of their break. They begin to identify with the generation that neighbors that of their children, rather than identifying with the older generation.

Likewise, children born as break babies may subconsciously shift to identifying with the generation closer to their parents in order to prevent the gap.

If a young Boomer in the generational break window has Millennial children, that Boomer may have more of a Gen X relationship with them. But if an old Millennial in the generational window has Boomer parents, then the Millennial might slide and the relationship between them will be more Boomer/Gen X. The old Millennial may even have iGen children and act like a Millennial most of the time with most of their other relationships. It may be the generation they identify with the most, but that

Boomer/Gen X relationship will always remain with the parents. So, parent/child generational relationships are almost always conjoined, even if that means one or the other redefines themselves psychologically to prevent a generational gap.

Think of a teeter-totter or, as I grew up calling them, a see-saw. On one end you have someone of the Silent generation. On the other, you have that Silent's grandchild, a solid Millennial. In the middle, at the pivot, is the child/parent of the two. As the teeter-totter swings down to the Silent side, the person in the middle slides toward them, into a Baby Boomer relationship nearest the Silent. But as it swings the other way toward the Millennial, the person slides again through the break and into a Gen X relationship nearest the Millennial.

I have found this principle at work in the generational dynamic: there seldom exists a true generational gap. Where a perceived gap might exist, one or the other, usually the one closest to the break, will slide emotionally and psychologically in order to fill the role of the missing generation. What is so fascinating is that they might slide in both directions when necessary, and so develop an almost split personality that doesn't really fit well into either generation, because they change according to the generation of the people they are around at any given moment. They take on characteristics of both generations as needed.

For example, as I've already stated, I am a break baby.

To my parents, who are Baby Boomers, I act like a Gen Xer; but to my children, who are iGen, I act like a Millennial. As I age, and my identity becomes more defined by my children rather than my parents, I will continue to act more and more like a Millennial. Yet with my parents, I will probably always act like a Gen Xer.

Do you get it now? In many ways, a person's generation is less defined by the specific year they were born, but more in how they interact with the generations around them. So it becomes an emotional and psychological division rather than a black and white physical line drawn between one year and the next. It's the family dynamics a person is born into that define the generation with which a person most identifies.

> *In many ways, a person's generation is less defined by the specific year they were born, but more in how they interact with the generations around them.*

Know where you are on the generational timeline. Know where your parents are. Know where your children are. If there are generational gaps, those closest to the generational break window will most likely slide back and forth to fill that gap and take on characteristics of both generations.

This study is concerned mostly with the four most

influential generations in the church: the Silent Generation, Baby Boomers, Generation X, and Millennials.

The very young iGeneration will be discussed a little, but since they are still forming their impressions of the world, it is difficult to predict how they are going to interact with it. Also, the elderly GI Generation will not be discussed at length since this generation is becoming smaller and is less able to serve in the church.

On the next page is a chart of the dividing lines used in this book. Find yourself and those closest to you before we begin studying the characteristics of each generation.

GENERATIONAL DIVIDING LINES

Silent Generation
1928–1945

Baby Boomers
1946–1964

Generation X
1965–1982

Millennials
1983–2000

iGeneration
2000–Today

REFLECTION QUESTIONS

1. What generation are you? Your parents? Your children? Based on the "break baby" idea, also indicate what generation they are most likely to identify as.

2. Name some of your closest friends and identify the generations they are in. Indicate if any of them are in the break.

3. When reflecting on conflict, what patterns might be generationally influenced?

CHAPTER 3

THE SILENT GENERATION

1928–1945

(a.k.a. Traditionalists or Builders)
As of 2017, they are between 72 and 89.

WHO ARE THEY?

This generation was born into the world of the Great Depression, hard times, low incomes, and general poverty. The oldest are too young to remember the Crash of '29 but were raised in the shadow of its impact, which would later need a world war for the economy to recover. They lived during the discovery of Pluto as a planet and probably still refuse to believe those who now call it something else. They saw the imprisonment of Al Capone and the death of Bonnie and Clyde, the flights of Amelia Earhart and the tragedy of the Lindbergh baby. They saw the splitting of the atom and the development of atomic weapons. Prohibition came to a reluctant halt, putting an end to illegal speakeasies. The Empire State Building, the

Golden Gate Bridge, and the Hoover Dam were all completed during the early years of this generation.

In the entertainment industry, they saw the premier of Snow White, the first appearance of Superman in the comic books, and held their breath in panic as Orson Welles read the H.G. Wells novel *War of the Worlds* on the radio in 1938. They witnessed the helicopter invented, the Jeep invented, the t–shirt invented, the ballpoint pen invented, the microwave invented, the slinky invented, and near the end of the generation's birth range, the first computer was built. Television made its debut in 1936 with the broadcast of the opening ceremony of the Olympic Games in Berlin.

They grew up in the most stable home environment of any generation...

Finally, from 1939 to 1945, the United States fought the Second World War. While in the final year of the war the youngest of this generation were born, the oldest of this generation endured most the war from home during their formative years; as parents, uncles, older brothers, relatives, and neighbors went to fight, and the women of the family went to work. Many of the oldest in this generation went to work with them or were given the responsibility of maintaining the homestead.

Sometimes called the "Lucky Few," they grew up in the most stable home environment of any generation, immediately following the turmoil of the depression and the war.[4] They benefited not only from stable homes but stable economies and relative world peace. Those that followed the previous generation into military service served less time in less volatile environments with extremely low casualty rates, and they were able to draw the same veteran's benefits as those who had risked more. At times, they enjoyed nearly 100% job fulfillment, with plenty of white-collar jobs for everyone. Women married younger than in any other generation, were more educated, and were inspired to work in their own pink-collar jobs, partly thanks to the influence of Rosy the Riveter during the war. This generation came of age in the shadow of the GI Generation, their heroes, who were mostly over-protective in raising them because of the world instability they endured.

Being a post-WWII generation, Silents are extremely patriotic. They can also be ambitious, seeking power and status as a subconscious way to prove themselves to their parent generation. Stuck between the heroes of the GI Generation and the free-spirits of the Baby Boomers, there was no room for them to rise or be set free into their own strong identity. They became instead a generation of stability, of following the rules, of staying the course, and of living life in a relatively unexciting, extremely traditional, and stable manner, as their efforts effectively

---

[4] Elwood Carlson, *The Lucky Few: Between the Greatest Generation and the Baby Boom* (Dordrecht: Springer, 2008).

built the intellectual, emotional, and structural foundation for the generations to come.

CHARACTERISTICS[5]

Defining Characteristic
Stability

The Silent generation does not like change, does not like to relocate, and does not like the status quo of their lives to be challenged. They want to carry on as they've always done, to do their patriotic duty, to prove to their parents that they have what it takes to keep the country going and to provide consistency for their free-spirited children. They want family, friendships, work relationships, jobs, and homesteads to remain consistent; and as a result, they are extremely loyal to people and places that give them an identity. They were raised to be survivors and savers, and are process planners when it comes to something new.

Everything about them and their broader characteristics carry the base characteristic of stability.

Strengths
Dependable. When given a task, they will do it without much fuss, without much to-do, and without the

---

[5] Chris Adams, ed., *Women Reaching Women*, rev. ed. (Nashville: Lifeway Press, 2005), 31-34.

expectation of reward. They will do it thoroughly, not stopping until the job is done right. They are people of their word and hard working. They enjoyed overall generational success due to their work ethic; small generation population and low work competition; and a stable and growing economy. They are financially stable and have enjoyed freedom of career in all occupations, which made them leaders in business, industry, and the creative arts.

Caring. They delight in nothing more than pouring affection on others because they themselves enjoy receiving affection. They understand that the world is not made by doing and going, but by the family and friends you have along the way. Those who attended college tended to have preferred more nurturing careers, such as education or medicine.

Inclusiveness. "We are all in this together." Growing up with the memory of the Great Depression and the reality of the Second World War, this generation knew more than the previous generation that all people can be affected, regardless of race or social status. As adults, they championed equal rights for all citizens and led desegregation.

Weaknesses

Traditional. Having been reared over-protected by the post-World War II GI Generation, they are low risk takers and conformists. Despite being ambitious, they generally are not innovators. They stood on the shoulders of the innovative giants of the GI Generation and didn't quite understand the free-spirit innovators of the Baby Boomers. They'll do things the way they know, the way that's been proven to them as effective, and they'll spend very little time thinking of ways to improve upon the process. Though many Silents rose to the top of their professions and careers through their ambition, they did so by staying the course, working hard, being consistent in their production, and not straying too far from the status quo. They eventually took charge of industries because they had proven themselves trustworthy and to be fair, impartial, and calm leaders.

Stubborn. Silents value stability and dependability. They will cling to this as long as possible. If anything threatens their stability, they instinctively reject it and fight against it. Many times the desire for stability can be stronger than logic. It can be shocking how far they will go to protect this stability.

Poor parents. Because of the over-protection of their parents, they raised the most under-protected generation of the century. They took their caring strength to a fault many times. They had high rates of abortion, divorce, and percentages of mothers working outside the home by choice rather than necessity; all of which led to a high rate of latchkey children. Members of this generation were leading developers of mid-century film and TV pornography, founding both Playboy and Penthouse. In the late 60s and early 70s members of this generation were prominent leaders in the women's liberation movement.

SPIRITUAL HERITAGE

The Great Depression brought financial struggles to the church but also forced congregations to rely more on each other and to think outwardly about helping their fellow man.[6] Radio services became popular, and the church, in general, saw a re–strategizing and a restructuring to keep with the new financial dynamic. As World War II raged, the church became a constant anchor for everyone looking for something to transcend their problems and create some form of stability in their lives.[7] Silents went to church because everyone they knew did, it was a part of life, a part of their family, and they couldn't imagine anything different. They needed it, for support and encouragement in those tough times. Without the church, there was no constant in life.

Fundamentalists withdrew into the shadows,

---

[6] "Religion 1931-1939," Encyclopedia.com, http://www.encyclopedia.com/article-1G2-3424800073/religion-1931-1939.html (accessed April 13, 2016).

[7] "W.W. II Brought Americans Back to Church," Old Magazine Articles, http://www.oldmagazinearticles.com/WW2-church-attendance-American-church-attendance-increased-during-world-war-two#.Vul_lkfuMY8 (accessed April 13, 2016); "America During WW II: Churches," Children In History, http://histclo.com/country/us/chron/940/ww2/home/ww2us-church.html (accessed April 13, 2016).

preferring to wait on the wrath of God upon the world; and with World War II, they thought God's wrath had come. After the war, church attendance and religious importance skyrocketed, with 49% of Americans claiming weekly attendance in the 50s, and 70% of Americans claiming that religion was in important part of their daily lives throughout the 50s and 60s.[8] The 1940s saw a surge in Pentecostalism as the Latter Rain Movement and Healing Revivals swept across the nation.

Yet the church struggled to reconcile with intellectual liberalism and the growing popularity of ideas like universalism, evolution, and deism. This caused many denominations to adopt liberal theologies. As a result, the line between religious business and duty, and true relational Gospel began to blur.

When Silents began to find leadership in the church, the programs implemented to sustain the church after the war were perpetuated and made stable, often showing little change in methodology and ministry technique until the Boomers began to come of age. Instead, Silents brought a business-like management to the church

---

[8] Frank Newport, "Questions and Answers about Americans' Religion," Gallup, http://www.gallup.com/poll/103459/questions-answers-about-americans-religion.aspx (accessed April 13, 2016).

Spiritual Worldview[9] –

Objective Theism – Shaped by the stability of their lives, the importance of the consistency of God, and church experiences post-depression and during the war, Silents often believe **God is objectively consistent in dealing with each person.** God, and by extension the church, doesn't change. They view the world, their relationship with God, and their experience with the church through this lens.

Truth Statement – *"My truth is the only truth."* Silents don't want to compromise on truth values. Even if what they hold to be the truth is merely a social construct or a tradition of their upbringing they still hold it to be the only acceptable truth.

For example, when faced with two opposing ideas, the Silents will struggle to understand how any idea other than their own could possibly exist. It won't make sense to them how someone could think differently.

Let's take a very simple scenario, perhaps overly simple, but enough to give you an idea of how this generation thinks. We'll use this same scenario with every

---

[9] The Spiritual Worldview and Truth Statements found in this study for each generation are of my own invention as an attempt to summarize philosophically what we know about each generation through their characteristics.

generation so that you can see the differences.

Think about a simple matter of choosing what to have for dinner. You want chicken, but the Silent wants tacos. When the conflict happens, the Silent might respond, "But we always have tacos on this night. Why should we change to chicken?"

My truth is the only truth.

Ministry challenges – As this generation ages and dies, churches will lose their strongest tithers, their most loyal participants, and the original builders of older, but successful church programs. However, they are often unwilling to adapt to modern strategies of ministry that might promote renewed church health. Their loyalty to the traditional church structure, order, and practices can create significant friction with younger generations.

REFLECTION QUESTIONS

1. Who do you know in the Silent generations?

2. What positive traits do you observe?

3. What negative traits do you observe?

4. How are they typical or not typical of the generational characteristics described in this chapter?

CHAPTER 4

THE BABY BOOMERS

1946–1964

As of 2017, they are between 53 and 71.

WHO ARE THEY?

The war is over. Things are changing fast. The economy is better than it's ever been, and families are leaving the city to settle into suburban neighborhoods, to build their dream homes and dream lives. Beginning in 1946, a baby was born in the United States on an average of one every 8 seconds, 11,000 a day, 4 million a year for the next 18-20 years.[10] The children of the Silent Generation largely lacked for nothing, were given a greater freedom from parental involvement, and were more lavishly spoiled than their parents. They reaped the benefits from the stability and provisional growth created

---

[10] Bill Craig and Donna Gandy, *Respect: Meaningful Ministry with Baby Boomers in Your Church and Community* (Nashville: Lifeway Press, 2009), 10.

by their grandparents and perpetuated by their parents, and they took advantage of life in ways the other generations could not imagine.

Modernization was also upon the nation. TVs quickly replaced radios in every home, and the words "It's Howdy Doody time!"[11] became a call to come running into the family room. Kitchens came standard with microwaves during the 70s, and every home had at least one vehicle. Baby Boomers were the first generation to grow up with Dr. Seuss, Disney, Alfred Hitchcock, Johnny Carson, and James Bond. As they came of age, Wal-Mart, the birth control pill, and credit cards became a part of their daily life.

To the Baby Boomers, Queen Elizabeth has always been Queen of England, Fidel Castro had always been dictator of Cuba, and Presidential candidates have always debated on television. The oldest can remember the Korean War, but all of them remember the Cold War when nuclear tension gripped the world. Families were installing fallout shelters, and Bert the Turtle taught every child to sing "duck and cover."[12]

But Bert the Turtle could not save John F. Kennedy, Marilyn Monroe, or Martin Luther King, Jr. Neither could their peaceful ambitions keep many Baby Boomers from

---

[11] "The Howdy Doody Show." IMDB. http://www.imdb.com/title/tt0165594 (accessed April 13, 2016).

[12] "Duck And Cover," IMDB, http://www.imdb.com/title/tt0213381/ (accessed April 13, 2016).

flying across the world to serve in Vietnam, a war that was not theirs. Sent by a country who did not appreciate them, they saw and did things no one who hadn't been there themselves could ever understand. Protests, riots, draft dodging, Woodstock, rock 'n roll, drugs, and the sexual revolution were all a part of their daily lives.

Boomers grew up while their parents, the Silents, started fighting the barriers of racial segregation. Yet while we tore down walls in America, Russia put up its own wall through the heart of Berlin. Then the whole world turned its eye toward space and the moon, and the quest to be the first to set foot on the lunar surface. In pursuit of the space race, NASA brought us lasers and Velcro.

As early Boomers became teenagers in the mid and late 60s, they flocked to the counterculture, becoming hippies, neo-Hinduists, pacifists, feminists, practicing free love and a variety of drugs. Anything and everything that rejected the status quo of society became an attraction to them.

Baby Boomers worshiped Muhammad Ali, Elvis, the Beatles, and the Rolling Stones, who would record what could be called the Baby Boomer generational anthem, "I Can't Get No Satisfaction." For in truth, that's the very worldview that shaped the Baby Boomers. The world was not satisfied with anything. Democracy or Communism? Segregation or integration? Frivolous sex or family? Credit or cash? Parenthood or abortion? Or perhaps merely a thirst to be first in everything, to have things their way or no way at all?

So the Baby Boomers grew with that mentality. Me first...masters of their own destiny...always seeking something bigger and better...always asking "What's in it for me?" and never quite being satisfied with anything. As they aged, they poured this dissatisfaction into their careers, using an education level greater than their parents to become vast innovators – turning hobbies into world-changing careers in technology and laying the foundation for the digital age. Baby Boomers brought us Microsoft, Apple, and the World Wide Web.

They were spenders not savers. Often accused of being overly materialistic, Boomers created a surge of national household debt. Now as they face retirement, they don't want to retire at the previously accepted age of 60.[13] Many can't retire since they neglected to prepare financially for their later years. They don't want to or financially can't pass the baton. They will be the largest, longest living generation in American history because of enormous medical advancements.

---

[13] Craig & Gandy, 11-13.

CHARACTERISTICS[14]

Defining Characteristic
Control

In every aspect of their lives, Baby Boomers want to be in charge. "The only way to get something done right is to do it yourself." When control of their world is threatened, Boomers fight back. They won't let their personal destiny be determined by anyone else. Even in death, they seek to maintain control as they are the first generation to be advocates of the living will.

Everything about them, their broader characteristics and actions, carries with them the base characteristic of control.

Strengths

Social – They enjoy personal interaction with others. They tend to be more drawn to larger social activities, whereas the other three generations discussed in this study tend to enjoy smaller intimate gatherings.

Youthful perspective on life – Boomers refuse to grow old gracefully like their parents and want to remain "cool." They are more likely to buy fancy cars in their retirement or try to return to the "glory days" of their youth through their hobbies.

---

[14] Adams, 37.

Self-sufficient – "I can handle it myself." Boomers can and want to handle all their daily activities themselves and will generally try to solve a problem without help before seeking professional advice.

<u>Weaknesses</u>

Self-seeking – They want what they want when they want it bigger, better, and now. Their happiness is more materialistic in nature; and by satisfying their cravings immediately, they gain some measure of that happiness.

Vanity – They can be obsessed with appearances, physical or social, and will go above and beyond to make themselves, the people around them, and their environment have the appearance they want others to see.

Strong-willed – Their way or no way. They can be difficult to convince of new methods and strategies or new routines. Unlike the Silents, this is not an issue of stability and challenge of that stability, but rather it is an affront to their control of the issue. If it is not their idea or they can't take charge of it, then they don't want it.

SPIRITUAL HERITAGE

Forced to go to church as children, to listen to church teachings opposed to the world they lived in, many Boomers abandoned church to seek their own destiny and to take control of their own spiritual lives; some sought spiritual self-worth in eastern mysticism or physical pleasures. Most that were raised in church eventually came back when they had families of their own. They finally recognized the value of their spiritual upbringing and wanted to provide the same values for their children.

Quickly taking leadership roles and keeping them, Boomers became some of the most active church-goers ever. Today 61% of Protestant pastors, 58% of lay leaders, and 50% of the tithers are all Boomers.[15]

> *God provides individual experiences to each person.*

Spiritual Worldview – *Individualistic Theism* – Shaped by their experiences, their desire for control of their lives, and how they sought and found their own spiritual identity, Boomers believe **God provides individual experiences to each person**. They view the world, their relationship with God, and their experience with the church through this lens.

Truth Statement – *"My truth is better than your truth."* Boomers don't want to give control to other truths. They see them as inferior and unable to meet their needs. Rather, they try to force their truth value on others.

For example, when faced with two opposing ideas, the Boomer will claim their own idea as superior.

Thinking about dinner again, if a Boomer wants tacos and you want chicken, the Boomer might respond, "Tacos

---

[15] Adams, 35.

are better, so we're having tacos. Period."

> *My truth is better than your truth.*

<u>Ministry challenges</u> — Transitioning Boomers out of leadership roles is perhaps the biggest challenge the church faces in the coming years. Boomers are refusing to let the younger generations take the baton and in many cases even refusing to train them. In places where Boomers feel like they are losing control, they are simply leaving the church because it goes against their nature to watch things being done differently than they would do it.[16] When unable to take control and do it "their way," they begin to seek that control in other places. Where change comes at the expense of their personal fulfillment or control, change is opposed. Yet without passing the baton, without training their replacements, there are no future leaders to take the reins of the church.

Boomers also constitute the largest percentage of tithers. Losing the Boomer generation AND the Silent generation over the course of the next 50 years will drastically alter the financial landscape of the church.

---

[16] Adams, 37.

REFLECTION QUESTIONS

1. Who do you know in the Boomer generations?

2. What positive traits do you observe?

3. What negative traits do you observe?

4. How are they typical or not typical of the generational characteristics described in this chapter?

CHAPTER 5

GENERATION X

1965–1982

(a.k.a. Baby Busters)
As of 2017 they are between 35 and 52

WHO ARE THEY?

Elder Gen Xers remember the 70s as children and the 80s as teenagers. Younger Gen Xers remember the 80s as children and the 90s as teenagers. These three decades span the formation of the worldview of Gen Xers, with special attention to the 80s which both halves share.

The 70s saw the unstable world of the 60s slowly disintegrate and find some form of stability by the early 80s. The Vietnam War came to a lack-luster end, eventually resulting in South and North Vietnam uniting into one country. The cold war began to ebb away, culminating in Reagan's famous challenge to Gorbachev to tear down the Berlin wall. What began in the 60s as a technology revolution, continued into the 70s with the introduction of the VCR, floppy disc, the pocket calculator, the Sony Walkman, and the founding of Microsoft. Technology would continue to boom throughout the 80s and 90s bringing us to a modern technological state unlike anything history has ever seen. The 80s brought us the personal computer, cell phones, video games, and CDs, all of which found perfection and continued to be reinvented throughout the 90s until today. Xers are therefore known as the generation of MTV, video games, and the internet.

Medical science brought test tube babies, DNA mapping, and the identification of AIDS. Roe vs. Wade legalized abortion in the early 70s when the oldest Gen Xers were still children, and in 1997, Dolly became the first cloned sheep when the youngest Gen Xers were getting ready for college.

The entertainment industry went through another Golden Age with Michael Jackson's *Thriller*, George Lucas, Stephen Spielberg, Star Wars, ET, Indiana Jones, Rambo, Rocky, and the Terminator.

Gen Xers remember the explosion of the Challenger, the meltdown at Chernobyl, the finding of the Titanic, and the Exxon Valdez oil spill. They watched as Diana lived the fairytale dream, marrying her prince and becoming a real princess. Then they saw her die.

In the 90s, elder Gen Xers entered their mid-20s and younger Xers became teens. During this time the Soviet Union fell, Desert Storm liberated Kuwait, and apartheid laws were struck down in South Africa. Domestic terrorism began to rise with the bombing of the World Trade Center and the Oklahoma City Federal Building. Xers watched the standoff in Waco and the Rodney King riots in LA, and they held their breath to find out if OJ was innocent or guilty.

Gen Xers saw the breakdown of social barriers across the board. During their formative years, everything that was once taboo became accepted or was challenged: racism, women's rights, Native American rights, and gay and lesbian rights. The events of their generation led them to have "situational ethics," truth that is in the eyes of the beholder. In matters of right and wrong, gray areas covered what was once black and white. Their perception is that absolute truth and morality no longer exist in the United States.

They are disillusioned with institutions, having seen the failed marriages of their parents, employers' disrespect of their parents, and the religious hypocrisy from their parents. They have delayed marriage, bounced from job to job, and often searched for truth by combining the more pleasing elements of religions.

As a result, a rift exists between them and the Boomer Generation, where the Boomers railed against the Xers for their worthlessness and laziness, and Xers—seeing the futility in the lives of the Boomers—had no desire to be like them.

The dominant worldview of Gen Xers and all who

come after them is Postmodernism. While the virtues and vices of Postmodernism are vast and complex, a key issue that defines the worldview of this generation is relativism…meaning all truth is subjective and individualistic. In other words, there are no absolutes.[17]

CHARACTERISTICS[18]

Defining Characteristic
Respect

Xers champion respect for themselves first, then respect for others. They care about tolerance for diverse ideas and opinions and seek acceptance of those ideas and opinions. Attitudes that promote exclusivity or low tolerance according to race, religion, sexual preference, or any other division will push them away. However, showing a person respect and worth will go a long way to bridging this gap.

Strengths

Adventurous – Xers are not afraid to try new things, to leave behind what has worked in the past, and to press forward with something new and refreshing. They are

---

[17] Gene Edward Veith, *Postmodern Times: A Christian Guide to Contemporary Thought and Culture*, Turning Point Christian Worldview Series (Wheaton, Ill.: Crossway Books, 1994).

[18] Adams, 39-41.

willing to experiment and take risks, sometimes failing spectacularly, but also succeeding in huge ways.

Technological – They are very adept at multimedia and computer technology. They are out-of-the-box problem solvers partly because they refuse to think like their parents and partly because they grew up honing problem-solving skills via video games. They have also become adept at doing multiple things at once: reading, listening to music, talking, and watching TV without losing their train of thought. Again, this may be a characteristic that can partly be credited to growing up with video games where hand-eye coordination, music, video movement, and sometimes partnership and conversation were required to solve problems.

Family minded – Those who began families care deeply for and protect their families. They value close relationships with friends and family, and this generation slowed the rate of divorce and abortion seen in the previous two generations.[19]

Weaknesses

Low self-esteem – Xers as a whole are emotionally weakened by being perceived as slackers and whiners by older generations. This drove many to live an amoral lifestyle and to reject the traditional family and religious paradigms of their parents. They also have the highest incarceration rate. They may be challenged, enraged, or

---

[19] Adams, 40.

sometimes defeated by the Boomers, depending on how individual personalities handle criticism. Those defeated may still live at home with their parents, those enraged have strained relationships, and those challenged are constantly seeking to prove themselves to and succeed above their parents.

Attractional – Xers are always seeking that next thrill or the next attractional item to bring them happiness and a sense of self-worth. They struggle to find happiness in long-term endeavors. They are emotional thrill seekers, and when the novelty wears off, they move on. Many struggle to keep long-term jobs as a result.

Low tolerance for self-failure – If an Xer is unable to obtain his or her goal or perform up to the expectations placed upon them, they may move on to something else that they can do without being criticized. Many Gen Xers are highly educated. However, those who felt like a college education would be too difficult, or perhaps were simply not attracted to furthering their education, did not even attempt it.

SPIRITUAL HERITAGE

Gen Xers who attended church as children were mostly forced to attend by their Boomer parents who had returned to church after rebelling. Boomers did not always seek genuine relational Christianity but expected the church to provide that for their family. Many Xers saw high levels of hypocrisy and spiritual compromise in the home and Sunday morning religion in the church. As a result, a genuine relationship with Christ was not a clear teaching from their parents, and family discipleship was mostly missing. The church became to them an unnecessary mask, and many Xers left the church as soon as they were old enough. They sought a Postmodern religious identity that they could claim as their own apart from their parents' idea of religious identity. Today they are the most missing generation in the church.[20]

Spiritual Worldview – *Postmodern Respect* – Shaped by the condescending views of society upon their generation and the prevailing cultural movement of Postmodernism, Xers believe that **other people's views about God are worth respecting**. They are tolerant of other people's religious views and ideas of right and wrong, and they respect people who have different ideas from their own. They view the world, their relationship with God, and their experience with the church through this lens.

Other people's views about God are worth respecting.

---

[20] Adams, 39; George Barna, *The Second Coming of the Church* (Nashville: Word Pub., 1998), 75.

Generation X | 43

Truth Statement – *"I will respect your truth if you respect mine."* They want their truth values respected, even though they don't expect older generations to adopt them. In turn, they offer respect for the truth values of others.

For example, when faced with two opposing views, the Gen Xer will concede the worth of the other person's idea and give them respect for it, but he or she will also expect the other person to do the same until they can come to an agreement.

I will respect your truth if you respect mine.

Back to the question of dinner, if an Xer wants tacos and you want chicken, the Xer might reply, "You can have chicken if you want, but I'm eating tacos."

Ministry challenges – Xers are the most missing generation in the church and the most difficult to reach. Over-hyping church programming in an attempt to get them involved in "religious activities" will turn them away. Aggressive evangelism is more likely to push them away because they feel it disrespects a person's personal religious convictions. Dogmatic beliefs that are more traditional or inferred from scripture rather than specifically prescribed in scripture are seen as hypocritical.

Xers who get involved in church are more likely to do so as they age, have settled down into the family, and have established a self-worth spiritual identity apart from their parents. Xers who are still young, single, and struggling to find an identity not defined by their parents are unlikely to come to church. Because they are attractional-minded, if a church does not have all the "bells and whistles" they will use that as an excuse not to come. They are not afraid to drive long distances to find a church that suits their tastes.

However, it is estimated that only one out of seven attend church at all.[21] Because of their overall absence and inconsistency, Gen Xers are the weakest tithers.

---

[21] Thom S. Rainer, "The Buster Generation," *Leading Adults*, Winter 2003-2004, 26-27.

REFLECTION QUESTIONS

1. Who do you know in Generation X?

2. What positive traits do you observe?

3. What negative traits do you observe?

4. How are they typical or not typical of the generational characteristics described in this chapter?

CHAPTER 6

MILLENNIALS

1983–2000

(a.k.a. Gen Y or Bridgers)
As of 2017, they are between 17 and 34.

WHO ARE THEY?

The history which shaped the Millennials is not too different from that of the young Xers. They grew up in a technologically advanced world that celebrated inclusion and condemned all forms of exclusion. Elder Millennials were children in the late 80s, most probably too young to remember the Challenger explosion, but they all remember the Columbia disaster.

If any were paying attention to the news they might remember the fall of the Berlin wall and the Exxon Valdez oil spill. Those two specific events would become the foundation of how the worldview of the Millennials would be shaped: the Berlin wall representing the tearing down of social barriers and championing of social justice, and the oil spill representing a heightened sense of eco-friendliness.

If a cause is worth fighting for, Millennials will fight for it, they will support it, and they will rally others to the cause.

Clinton, George W. Bush, and Obama are the only presidents they really remember. Many of their parents went to Kuwait for Desert Storm; and to Millennials, Islamic radicals have always been the enemy of the United States. They all watched in horror from their classrooms as the Twin Towers burned and fell, many of them seeing the second plane crash live. Terrorism became the enemy, and, by extension, it became a representation of the evils of all organized religion.

They are a generation that has never *not* known advanced technology. To them, a cell phone that couldn't txt was old…and, why would anyone ever plug a phone into the wall? smh ;) They've been on Facebook since Facebook began. They've been surfing YouTube since YouTube began. "Google" has always been a verb, and if you really want to know the truth of something, just check Wikipedia.[22] The world became infinitely small, with the ability to video call anyone around the world at any time. Life before the internet is unfathomable. Life without technology is unimaginable.

What sets Millennials apart emotionally from the Gen Xers, is that they are the children *of* Gen Xers. As such,

---

[22] https://en.wikipedia.org/wiki/Wikipedia

they did not grow up with the stigma of failure that many Gen Xers endured at the hands of Baby Boomers. Millennials grew up feeling like respect, inclusion, and acceptance was the normal way of life. They are the first generation to play sports that did not keep score, where every child was a winner, and which made allowances for physically challenged children to be a part of everything any other child could do.

Racism is a completely foreign concept because to exclude someone for any reason, especially something as trivial as skin color, seems as ancient as cavemen. For the first time, bullying became a social problem while older generations bemoaned a lack of "thick skin."

Political correctness took on a life of its own.

In other words, Millennials took the Postmodern idea of "truth is relative to the person" to another level, saying that "your truth should be important to me," not just accepted or respected. If your cause is important to you and you are important to them, then your cause is important to them and they will make it their cause too.

CHARACTERISTICS[23]

Defining Characteristic
Inclusion

Millennials grew up in a world where everyone had a place and separation for any reason was frowned upon. They value inclusion for themselves, their families, their friends, their communities, and any other area of their lives. Where Xers want everyone to show respect for everyone else, this is not necessarily inclusion. Millennials want that extra step, and want everyone to be included in everything, regardless of race, gender, or sexual preference. This is good on the one hand because it better reflects the mentality of Jesus in outreach. It is bad on the other hand because Millennials tend to create superficial relationships for the sake of inclusion and are sometimes known for collecting friends as one might collect stamps.

Everything about them, their broader characteristics and actions, carries with them the base characteristic of inclusion.

Strengths
Accepting – As inclusionists, Millennials are very quick to accept someone regardless of their past or background. There are no barriers for a Millennial and no reasons why anyone should be exclusive of anyone else.

---

[23] Adams, 42.

Community minded – Millennials recognize the value of helping others, for healing social problems, and building community harmony.

Freethinkers – Millennials will not be told how to think. They want to be free to make up their own minds and make their own informed decisions. They are naturally suspicious of any authority figure and tend to question everything. However, they are willing to accept different opinions in time and with ample convincing.

Bonus: Optimistic – This is not a strength indicator by itself, but is an outgrowth of all of the above. By being openly accepting, community minded, and free thinkers, they seem to have a highly optimistic view of life and how life could be in a perfect world. They will use their strengths to try to accomplish that goal and to influence other generations to do the same.

Weaknesses

Materialistic – They want the best of everything. They will spend extra money for something more extravagant. They will discard something that is perfectly good in order to "upgrade" to something newer, faster, and better. They are not known as frugal savers.

Selfish –They are inherently selfish about what goes on around them. They are accepting of everyone, so long as you agree with THEIR definition of "accepting." Everything should be for their benefit and their pleasure. They do not practice inclusion because it's right, but because it makes them feel like they're doing the right thing. They don't help the community for the community but ultimately for their own sense of self-worth. In the end, if a project or idea has no intrinsic value for them personally, they will not get involved.

Disrespectful – Millennials show respect, tolerance, and inclusion for all individuals on the outside but have little respect for those who do not agree to their definition of respect, tolerance, and inclusion. Consequently, older generations with different worldviews, who do not agree with what a Millennial might stand for, are given very little respect, and their ideas and values are rejected.

SPIRITUAL HERITAGE

The previous generation had almost forsaken the church, and many Millennials were not brought up in the church in the same numbers as other generations. The Xers did not place a priority on the church, and they did not force a false priority on their children.

However, the Millennials do not take the experiences of the Xers as personal to them. Millennials come to church by choice for community and spiritual answers. They objectively evaluate the church for truth and inclusiveness, to make the decision of what's right for them.

Throughout their lives they have repeatedly seen figures of authority, even those in the church, fall from integrity, and so they naturally have a suspicion and hesitancy with giving others authority in their lives. They approach the church much the same way, wishing to keep final authority with themselves rather than give over authority to a central figure such as a pastor. Make no mistake though, Millennials can be very spiritual people, they just might not always be the most religious–because to them institutional religion is not true Christianity.

> *Other people's views about God are worth consideration for including with their own.*

Spiritual Worldview – *Postmodern Inclusion* – Shaped by their inclusionary mentality and the prevailing cultural movement of Postmodernism, Millennials believe that **other people's views about God are worth consideration for including with their own**.[24] They accept that right and wrong are determined by the individual but are also willing to adopt another person's views of right and wrong. They view the world, their relationship with God, and their experience with the church through this lens.

Truth Statement – *"Your truth value is important to me if it is compatible with mine."* Truths are adopted and championed by Millennials, even if it is not their own. But

---

[24] Adams, 42.

if it deviates too far from their own accepted truth, it is quickly dismissed and ignored.

For example, when faced with two opposing views, the Millennial will evaluate the opposing view versus their own. If adequate compatibility is found, then the Millennial combines the two views into one, giving them equal and inclusive value and presenting the new idea as a compromise to be accepted by everyone involved.

Your truth value is important to me if it is compatible with mine.

Let's revisit dinner one more time. If a Millennial wants tacos and you want chicken, the Millennial might reply, "Why can't we have both? Let's have chicken tacos."

Ministry challenges – As stated earlier, many Millennials are skeptical of authority, especially spiritual authority. Getting them to understand that church is under the authority of God and not any individual is tricky and hinges on making them understand that Christianity is about a relationship with Christ not a relationship to organized religion. Unfortunately, many churches give Millennials plenty of reason to reject the authority of God and a relationship with Christ, because so many churches have devolved into the leadership of man and the authority of traditional religion.

Millennials tend to view the old traditions of the

church as outdated but are willing to accept traditions that can be supported by scripture, so long as the church is also not afraid of modern progress. They easily see through consumerism and hype. Many think the church is too political, exclusive, old-fashioned, unconcerned with the world, and hostile to people of other views. Worldviews and social problems are important to them, and they want to see a church addressing these issues with Biblical honesty and humility. They believe the institutional church spends too much time on "unimportant little things," like sexual purity and other rules to be "holy," and would rather the church be honest about real life situations.

Millenials must be reached by the church. Not only do they represent the future leadership of the church, but this generation is actually a larger generation than the Baby Boomers. Strictly speaking, Millenials attend church in greater numbers than Xers, however percentage wise they are probably just as missing.

REFLECTION QUESTIONS

1. Who do you know in the Millennial generation?

2. What positive traits do you observe?

3. What negative traits do you observe?

4. How are they typical or not typical of the generational characteristics described in this chapter?

CHAPTER 7

THE IGENERATION

"But Jesus said, 'Let the children alone, and do not hinder them from coming to Me; for the kingdom of heaven belongs to such as these.'" Matthew 19:14

What about the iGeneration?

Children born after the year 2000 are considered iGeneration. At least that's the name being used in this book. That may not be the name that sticks in the years to come, though it seems to be the most popular name at this time. Other names you may encounter are Homeland Generation, Digital Generation, Generation Z, 2Ks (TwoKays), or Cyber Generation.

Much is not yet known about this generation, as most of them are still young and their impressions of the world are still being formed. They are a generation raised entirely on technology and non-traditional family values. Many have limited attention spans and have not been taught traditional social norms of ethics, respect, and conduct.

Most are the children of Millennials, who can be very protective parents and often defend their children to a fault by putting more value in their trust of their children than their trust of other adults. Many Millennial Christian families are parenting with "grace parenting," emphasizing positive reinforcements without the use of negative discipline.

When dealing with these parents, be careful not to criticize or attack their children in any way. State facts, not judgments. Never punish without permission. Offer suggestions for course correction only if asked. Deal with situations as a matter of policy, equally among the children, without singling any child out.

Some older iGen might have Gen X parents. These parents are generally very encouraging and accepting and have high expectations. They, by instinct, parent the way their parents did; but at the same time hate themselves for it and often over-compensate through a relaxed parenting attitude. They don't want to make the same parenting mistakes but sometimes overreact without thinking. They use traditional discipline, but only sparingly.

When dealing with these parents, show them and their parenting skills respect, even if you do not agree with them. Never accidentally indicate they are bad parents. Deal with situations by focusing on the positives, but be honest. When given the chance, they will try to meet and exceed your parenting expectations, especially if you are a Boomer.

Also, do not forget the generational gap principle talked about at the beginning of this book. Gen Xers with iGen children will cause a shift in the generational identity for the ones closest to the break. Older iGen children near the break, who have Xer parents, may begin to act like Millennials as they age. But if the iGen is firmly rooted away from the break, the Xer parent will begin to act more like a Millennial as the children age.

For example, I have already stated that I am in the break between Gen X and Millennial. Strictly speaking, I am a very young Gen Xer. When interacting with my parents we may always have a Boomer/Gen X relationship.

However, my children are both iGen. The oldest is close enough to the Millennial/iGen break that we might possibly develop a Gen X/Millennial relationship. But the youngest is firmly in iGen. With so much established iGen in the home, my wife and I have discovered that we are identifying more and more with Millennials as we age and our children mature, developing a Millennial/iGen relationship between us and our children.

EMERGING CHARACTERISTICS

Despite knowing little about this upcoming generation, there are some emerging characteristics being observed. How these characteristics will develop into adulthood is yet to be seen. But I think it's a fair assumption that some form of these characteristics will persist. How did I get this information? By observing my own children and their friends, talking with other parents of iGen children, and by talking with people who work with iGen children on a regular basis. This was not a scientific survey, nor may it even be universally accurate. But through all the conversations I've had with youth and children's ministers, along with my own observations as a parent of this generation, here are some emerging characteristics that seem to be common.

Tech Fluency

As stated above, this is a generation raised entirely on technology. Whereas young Xers experienced tech evolving into its modern form while they were still in college and Millennials absorbed it during grade school, these iGen have been living with it since the cradle. They are the first children, even toddlers, who can expertly navigate an iPad. They learned how to handle apps, what video chatting is all about, and how to stream their favorite shows *before* they learned to read in many cases.

By saying they are tech fluent, we are saying that they learned the language of technology from infancy in the same way they learned to speak. It is not a learned skill or a second language, it is a native tongue.

> *The language of technology is a native tongue.*

Individualism Celebrated

Gen Xers champion respect for all individuals, Millennials champion inclusion for all individuals, but both of these concepts are broad ideas. These broad ideas have evolved into this emerging characteristic. The iGeneration *celebrates* individualism. It's the next logical step in what the previous two generations have championed. Now that people are respected and included, people must be celebrated for their individual characteristics, likes, dislikes, hobbies, and ideas.

Take geek culture, for instance. It is something that's always been around. The Xer "geeks" just wanted to be respected for enjoying the things they do. Millennial "geeks" expected to be included in the "cool" crowd and cried out for social justice when they were not. But as the iGen ages, more and more geek culture IS cool, it is celebrated, it is a thing to be proud of. The same could apply to alternative lifestyles.

So it is with everything that makes a person unique. Each person's individualism is worth celebrating.

Integrated Online/Real Life relationships

When my son was nine, we moved two hours away from his best friend. They never missed a step. Technology allowed them to continue their relationship as if distance were no barrier. Even when that friend moved an additional twelve hours away, it made no change. When they get together in real-life, they pick up right where they left off online as if there never was a separation. When video chatting, they use no formal communication rituals that adults might use to end conversations, formalities adults have imported from telephone conversations. Instead, this generation treats virtual communication like it's simply a live, face-to-face conversation.

Online and real life relationships are completely integrated.

To the iGen, or at least the ones old enough to have online relationships, there is little difference between online life and real life. They can transition from one to the other seamlessly. Distances are no issue for them. Some Xers and Millennials might feel awkward when developing online and real life relationships as separate relationships and then trying to integrate them into the other part of their lives. This is not an issue for the iGeneration. To them, online and real life relationships are completely integrated. In fact, I would go so far as to say they don't even comprehend there's a difference in the two.

Unfortunately, this characteristic may prove to be more of a weakness than a strength, especially if they fail to take precautions in regards to people misrepresenting themselves online.

Instant gratification

More so than Millennials who tend to want things right away, iGen *expects* things right away. Most are being raised in environments that can afford many more opportunities and luxuries than their parents had and, as a result, they have come to expect the best to be available for them whenever they want it. They have trouble waiting and trouble saving money for things they want immediately.

Noncommittal/Lack of perseverance

iGen have trouble committing completely to a project or a skill. In a world of instant gratification, if a thing becomes difficult or stressful, they are quick to move on to something else. They are more likely to spread out their skills into a broad range of beginner or intermediate levels, but they struggle to persist into mastery.

External self-worth

Because of the celebration of individualism mixed with their integration of online and real life relationships, iGen tend to put the locus of their identity further away from themselves than previous generations. Their self-worth tends to be defined by the things around them: their hobbies, their likes, their friends, their families. Mix this with instant gratification and a tendency to be non-committal and you can easily see how they struggle to create definitions of self-worth for themselves.

REFLECTION QUESTIONS

1. Who do you know in the iGeneration?

2. What positive traits do you observe?

3. What negative traits do you observe?

64 | We Are One

GENERATIONAL OVERVIEW TABLE

Generation	Silent Generation	Baby Boomers	Generation X	Millennials	iGen
Years	1928-1945	1946-1964	1965-1982	1983-2000.	2000-Current
Worldview	Objective Theism	Individualistic Theism	Postmodern Respect	Postmodern Inclusion	?
Major Characteristic	Stability	Control	Respect	Inclusion	?
Truth Statement	My truth is the only truth.	My truth is better than your truth.	I will respect your truth if you respect mine.	Your truth is important to me if it is compatible with mine.	?
Strengths	Dependable Caring Inclusiveness Fortitude	Social Youthful Self-sufficient	Adventurous Technological Family minded	Accepting Community minded Freethinkers	?
Weaknesses	Traditional Stubborn Poor parents	Self-seeking Vanity Strong-willed	Low self-esteem Attractional Low tolerance for self-failure	Materialistic Selfish Disrespectful	?

CHAPTER 8

GENERATIONAL RELATIONSHIPS

"Do nothing from selfishness or empty conceit, but with humility of mind regard one another as more important than yourselves; do not merely look out for your own personal interests, but also for the interests of others." Philippians 2:3-4

Understanding how a generation thinks is only part of the puzzle. It's also equally important to understand how those generational characteristics interact with one another. This is where true application can be found because most of the issues that occur within a church happen when two generations interact. Being able to anticipate what those interactions might look like, and better yet train the people to anticipate those interactions, can go a long way to creating unity within the church.

Most of the interactions actually land on the possibility scale of being positive and harmonious. These we'll look at first. Though they may be mostly positive, it is important to pay attention to the nuances of the interactions and how the characteristics of each generation might manifest during the interaction.

The last two interactions that will be reviewed are typically volatile. These are the interactions that need to be watched carefully. The only things that will prevent these interactions from spinning out of control are proactive training from leadership and an open willingness to work through these issues on the parts of both generations involved.

POSITIVE INTERACTIONS

Silents VS Boomers

Silents and Boomers find common ground today, even though their early relationships were strained. The major characteristic of Silents is stability, and the major characteristic of Boomers is control. Control being a form of self-central stability, Boomers identify and work really well with establishing stability for the Silents.

Since Boomers fled the church, fled the ideals of the parent generation, and eventually returned to what was instilled in them as children by their parents, they now value and respect the ideas of the parent generation and work to perpetuate it. Silents, being an aging generation, are more than happy to have their child generation step up and continue to pursue and lead according to mutually shared values. The shift allows Boomers to give Silents a

Silents respect Boomers for returning back to the ideals of their parent generation.

break from work so long as Boomers continue to perpetuate the stability already established. Silents recognize the change in the Boomers and respect them for coming full-circle back to the ideals of their parent generation. So there is mutual respect, common ground, and common goals.

Let's go back to the example of dinner that we used earlier as we review generational interactions. Choosing dinner is not always so simple as stated in the earlier chapters. If more than one generation is involved in the choice, then both truth statements and sets of generational characteristics are in conflict. The conflict must resolve somehow, and we find that resolution in the unique way the generational characteristics interact.

So, what if a Silent wants tacos and a Boomer wants chicken?

> Silent: "It's taco night. Let's make tacos."
> Boomer: "I want chicken. Chicken's better."
> Silent: "But we always have tacos on this night, why should we change?" *(Notice the **stability**.)*
> Boomer: *(now conceding to the parent generation but still keeping **control**)* "Okay. How about I

> make you chicken tonight, and I'll make tacos tomorrow."
>
> The Silent feels they have been heard and their stability is being valued, so they concede to the change.

Silents VS Xers

The grandparent/grandchild relationship between the generations is always a strong one. Silents often recognize that Xers feel disconnected and disrespected by the Boomers because they saw first-hand how the Boomers took their own self-destructive path and then overcompensated as parents. Silents tend to respect Xers more easily than Boomers do, and they are quickly willing to give Xers the benefit of the doubt and to let them explain their ideas in detail. Silents are also willing to allow Xers to produce change, so long as it is adequately explained and does not threaten their stability.

Xers cling to their grandparent generation, wanting to develop a thriving relationship with them. They will seldom push them out of their stability. However, this relationship between Silents and Xers might not extend past blood relationship due to the fact that Xers hold family relationships highly and Silents feel little obligation to the grandchildren of other people. In which case, the relationship between Silents and Xers who are not related may look more like the relationship between Silents and

Boomers for elder Xers or Silents and Millennials for younger Xers. See those examples in those cases. Below, the interaction is assumed to be a blood relationship.

What about dinner?

The grandparent/ grandchild relationship is always strong.

> Silent: "It's taco night. Let's make tacos."
> Xer: "But I want chicken." *(Notice the defensive tone and the passive-aggressive cry for **respect**.)*
> Silent: "We always have tacos on this night, why should we change?" *(**Stability** is clearly expressed.)*
> Xer: "Because I haven't had chicken in a long time."
> Silent: *(suspecting the Xer's parents never gave the other chicken)* "Okay. If you want chicken, I'll fix you chicken."

Boomers VS Millennials

This is the second grandparent generational relationship. Boomers and Millennials work well together. Boomers will often embrace their grandchildren where a strained relationship with their own children exists. To a Boomer, if the Xer children will not fall in line, then all the wisdom of their generation will be passed on to their grandchildren. Often you see Boomers bringing Millennials into the family business where Xers have refused. Boomers want desperately to have a good relationship with Millennials since the relationship with the Xers is so strained. They will go above and beyond to present themselves as relevant to their grandchildren. Millennials, of course, enjoy the attention and enjoy teaching their grandparent generation new things. As they are included by the Boomers, they in turn accept the Boomer's way of thinking as worth including.

Back to dinner…

> Boomer: "It's taco night. *I'll* make tacos." *(Notice the **control**.)*
> Millennial: "I'd rather have chicken."
> Boomer: "Tacos are better. We're having tacos."
> Millennial: "What about chicken tacos? That way we both get what we want." *(Notice the **inclusion**.)*
> Boomer: *(eager to please the grandchild relationship)* "Chicken tacos it is."

Xers VS Millennials

This generational relationship also gets along well in most cases. There is little difference between younger Xers and elder Millennials, save being defined by either their parent generation or their child generation. Xers and Millennials have core values that are similar and work well together. Xers value respect for all people, Millennials value inclusion for all people. Whereas having respect does not mean inclusion, and inclusion does not mean respect, the two often go together. Any strain that may come between these generations is usually in this area, where different approaches to the same problem either lack the respect Xers are looking for or lack the inclusion that Millennials are looking for.

Unfortunately, they often have trouble explaining how they feel about things in person, both being generations of digital communication. However, they also share the post-modern worldview and understand the value of truth ideas that are not their own.

> Xer: "It's taco night. I want tacos."
> Millennial: "I think I'd rather have chicken."
> Xer: "You can have chicken if you want, but I want tacos." *(Notice the **respect** for the other idea, but the lack of inclusion.)*
> Millennial: "Why don't we make chicken tacos?" *(Notice the attempt at **inclusion**.)*
> Xer: "Okay, we can do chicken tacos. But I'm doing beef too because I want beef. We can do both."

> *Millennials and Xers struggle to communicate emotionally in person.*

This solution to the problem, depending on the personalities of the individuals, can either be positive or negative. Both generations have tried to get at the same answer but from different perspectives: the Millennials championing inclusion of ideas but the Xers merely expecting respect for both ideas. Now neither feel completely satisfied. The Millennial really wanted chicken, not chicken tacos; and if the Xer is cooking two things, it might as well be chicken. The Xer now feels like they have to do twice the work to make the Millennial happy and doesn't understand why the Millennial isn't. They both have problems voicing how they truly feel. Either it will all come out and be resolved to the satisfaction of both, or it will stay internalized and build a chip on both shoulders, eventually to come out anyway.

Communication is the key to the Xer/Millennial relationship. If they will communicate, then they generally work well together.

VOLATILE INTERACTIONS

The Generational Wound
Boomers VS Xers

The world began to change between the Boomers and the Xers with the digital revolution transforming and defining the upcoming generation. Boomers initially saw little life value in the digital ambitions of their children. The post-modern worldview was developing, and the Xers were being taught by society that truth was relative. They grew up believing respect should be given to everyone and that everyone's truth was worth respecting. But the Boomers refused to adopt this relative truth view. The things that the Xers felt important to them were not valued by the Boomers. Society, in general, began to lament the future generation.

Being a break baby, but slightly on the Gen X side of the break I actually remember being a young primary school student, hearing news reports on the worthlessness of Generation X, and wondering if that included me. It was such a strong sentiment that it made an impression I haven't forgotten.

The formative influencers of the Xers were the Boomers. If the parent Boomer shared society's opinion, and they often did, then a wound was created. After all, they were the ones directly responsible for raising this "worthless" generation.

Xers grew up trying to prove their worth, their value, and trying to earn respect, not just for themselves as individuals, but for the truth views of their generation. So it comes to the truth views of the Xers not being respected by the Boomers, and the Xers are desperate to make Boomers understand that all truth views are important. Xers and Boomers butt heads and argue as each are trying to force the other into a conflicting view.

> *Xers see establishments run by Boomers as hostile. Boomers don't understand what they've done.*

Now nearing retirement, Boomers are refusing to pass on what they've worked hard for to the Xers and are choosing to skip to the Millennials in many cases. Meanwhile, Xers are refusing to give in to the Boomers, seeking respect and success outside and away from their parent generation. Boomers see the absence of Xers and they don't understand why or what they've done, even though they often still will not listen and accept the views of the Xers. Xers see establishments run by Boomers as hostile environments that will reject their views and ideas…and that includes churches.

Now dinner gets messy.

> Boomer: "It's taco night. I'm making tacos."
> ***(Control.)***
> Xer: "But, I don't want tacos. I want chicken."
> Boomer: "Tacos are better. We're having tacos."
> Xer: "Why do you think tacos are better? I think chicken is better. I want chicken."
> ***(Respect.)***
> Boomer: "It doesn't matter what you want, we're having tacos."
> Xer: "YOU NEVER LISTEN TO ME! YOU NEVER…"

Well, you can fill in the rest of the argument. It's not really about dinner, anyway. It eventually ends with an explosive shouting match, where one or the other leaves in anger and the one remaining gets what they want. But the problem isn't solved. This will happen again.

The Oddity Gap
Silents VS Millennials

The Silent Generation came of age in the shadow of a world war and the greatest technological invention of the time was the microwave. The Millennials came of age at the dawn of the information age and have never known a time when there was no internet, email, or HDTV. To say these two generations don't understand each other is an understatement.

Silents view the Millennials as excessive, selfish, and unable to support themselves if the technology were to go away. Millennials view the Silents as old-fashioned, out of touch, and not understanding that the world is technologically advanced and it's not going away. Since Silents value stability, they are very reluctant to embrace such advanced ways of thinking that the Millennials live with every day. Silents dismiss Millennials as being too progressive.

> *Silents dismiss Millennials as progressive. Millennials dismiss Silents as irrelevant.*

Millennials value inclusion and any idea that does not support their "definition" of inclusion is rejected. Silents, however, are reluctant to be included in their technological, post-modern worldview. Millennials dismiss Silents as irrelevant.

The irony is that both of these generations share the inclusion characteristic, Silents as a strength indicator and Millennials as the major characteristic. The difference is that the Silents value inclusion of people and the Millennials value the inclusion of truth ideas.

Here, dinner gets awkward.

> Silent: "It's taco night. Let's make tacos."
> Millennial: "I think I'd rather have chicken."

> Silent: "But we always have tacos on this night. Why should we change?" ***(Stability.)***
>
> Millennial: *(Doesn't understand what the big deal is about change.)* "Why not? What does it hurt to change?"
>
> Silent: "Because this is the way we do things."
>
> Millennial: "What about chicken tacos? Will you consider that?" ***(Inclusion.)***
>
> Silent: *(Stares at them, wondering how this "chicken taco" solves the problem. They were talking about chicken OR tacos, not chicken tacos.)* "That's not the same thing. I thought you wanted chicken."
>
> Millennial: "I do, I just thought…"

And you can fill in the rest of the conversation as they talk in circles trying to get to the same place but never really understanding where the other is coming from. It eventually ends with each of them giving up frustrated, the Silent making tacos anyway and the Millennial making an excuse to leave and seek chicken somewhere else.

These hypothetical interactions demonstrate the stereotype of each generation and are only a start. People are incredibly complicated and interactions may vary for many reasons. Be aware that different personality types might express generational characteristics differently. Though most Silents and Boomers get along fine, two

Type A personalities who dig in their heels about stability and control might well cause problems.

This book does not include a breakdown of personality types and how they are manifested through the generational characteristics, though future editions might. Just be aware that personality does indeed affect how generational characteristics are presented when interacting with others.

What you're meant to take away from these hypothetical interactions are the nuances of how each generation brings their characteristics with them to the conversation and how those characteristics might serve to define their reactions in certain situations.

How might this apply to the church? Imagine that choosing dinner is more than a conversation example but is also a metaphor for traditional versus modern church methods.

The Silent prefers the stability of traditional church methods and the Boomer is perfectly comfortable perpetuating that stability. The Silent might even concede to an Xer's more modern desire, but not at the expense of their own stability. The Boomer loves to experiment with the Millennials, so long as they are allowed to maintain healthy control.

However, the Silent does NOT understand the Millennial church mentality at all. They'll argue in circles about tradition versus modern, each trying to get to the same place from different directions. Eventually, the

Silent is going to try to do what is stable to them anyway, and the Millennial may give up and leave the church.

Millennials prefer more modern methods even though they are not opposed to tradition. Since Millennials and Xers get along, you'll most likely find them together in a modern setting.

You will not, however, find a healthy population of Boomers and Xers in a church. When it comes to church methods, they will fight and the Xer will leave.

What are we left with? More traditional-minded churches mostly populated by Silents and Boomers, and more modern-minded churches mostly populated by Xers and Millennials.

To repeat my earlier sentiments…this is not how it should be. The generations can work together if they will learn how to communicate with one another.

It is possible for Silents and Millennials to understand each other, but it may require compromise on both parts. Silents need to value the opinions and desires of Millennials. Millennials need to respect the Silents' need for stability.

It is possible for Boomers and Xers to get along. Boomers need to learn to relinquish control and trust that an Xer can get the job done. Xers need to learn not to be so sensitive to the opinions of Boomers.

Take a moment and reread the verse at the beginning of this chapter.

REFLECTION QUESTIONS

1. Considering your own generation, what are your typical interactions like with someone of the Silent generation?

2. What are your typical interactions like with someone of the Boomer generation?

3. What are your typical interactions like with someone of Generation X?

4. What are your typical interactions like with someone of the Millennials?

CHAPTER 9

GENERATION CYCLES

"That which has been is that which will be, and that which has been done is that which will be done. So there is nothing new under the sun." Ecclesiastes 1:9

Everything that has been reviewed so far is on the smaller scale of understanding individuals within a certain generation. However, it is also important to get a much larger view of each generation's place in history, how each generation has affected history and been affected by history, and how the development of the church can be viewed alongside these generational developmental lines. We need this broader understanding to be able to prepare for the future, to recognize the patterns of generations in history, and to attempt to develop strategies based on how those patterns might continue.

William Strauss and Neil Howe put together a fascinating theory of generational cycles that show how every generation is influenced by the immediate historical events around them. In turn, that generation influences the next series of historical events. This repeats in a cyclic generational and historical pattern resulting in the recurrence of four generational archetypes and four historical eras.[25]

When properly understood and evaluated, this theory can give us significant insight into how the characteristics of each generation are formed and how that generation affects its cultural context. The influence of immediate historical events then shapes the personality of the next generation.

> *This theory can give us significant insight into how the characteristics of each generation are formed…*

This theory might help us predict the personalities of future generations as well as give us some general characteristics of future culture and events.

This theory is not meant to predict the future, but it is a way of understanding how generations and historical events unfold in a cycle on a broader scale. The scope of the study here is not concerned with understanding history or attempting to predict historical markers. The goal is to use the research of Strauss and Howe to further understand how each generation adopted the characteristics they have and how

---

[25] William Strauss and Neil Howe, *The Fourth Turning: An American Prophecy* (New York: Broadway Books, 1998.

we might possibly prepare for the future of the church.

THE CYCLE OF HISTORY[26]

History itself has a cycle. Strauss and Howe have theorized four specific historical mood eras, which they call **turnings**. Like a wheel, history is turning. This wheel is divided into four sections, each section leading to a cultural transition that leads into the next section, eventually to return back to the first section in endless historical repetition. Here are the four turnings as explained by Strauss and Howe:

High – Strong institutions and weak individualism.

High– The High is the first turning of the cycle. It is characterized by strong institutions, weak individualism, and a confident society. All of this is built by a middle-aged Hero generation (we'll get to these generational archetypes in a moment) that helps bring an end to the Crisis, the immediately preceding historical era. The stability of the High is perpetuated by a young adult Artist generation. Children who grow up in this environment are considered a Prophet generation with an idealist worldview.

---

[26] Strauss & Howe, 101-105.

Awakening – This second turning of the cycle comes at a time when those young Prophet idealists tire of the lack of individualism in society and begin to attack institutions. The Artist generation has continued to stabilize society, giving these young Prophets the opportunity and ability to champion individual thought and freedom. Children who grow up in this environment are considered a Nomad generation with a reactive worldview. Nomads have trouble establishing their own identity during this time of questioning cultural identities.

Awakening – Attack on institutions.

Unraveling – Institutions are weakest and individualism is strongest.

Unraveling – The third turning happens after the Awakening takes hold. Institutions are at their weakest and individualism is at its strongest. It is the opposite of a High, where society is no longer institutionally strong because the Prophets are enjoying the fruit of the Awakening and the young adult Nomads have been left to wander the culture seeking an identity not easily satisfied. Children who grow up in this environment are considered a Hero generation with a civic worldview.

Crisis – This fourth turning is a result of the Unraveling, where some form of social and cultural crisis grips society. Institutions are destroyed and rebuilt. The Hero generation are young adults, and they largely lead society to the High turning of the next era. Children who grow up during a Crisis turning are considered an Artist generation with an adaptive worldview.

Crisis – Institutions destroyed and rebuilt.

The Crisis turning then gives way back to a High turning, and thus the cycle repeats.

THE CYCLE OF GENERATIONS[27]

The four generational archetypes grow up in a specific turning and are therefore shaped by the events of that turning. They go on to shape other turnings as they age, according to their unique generational characteristics.

Prophet – Prophets are idealists. They look for the best in individuals and society, and they see institutionalism as a poor substitute for individualism. They are born at the end of a Crisis and are children of a High turning. They have not experienced what's it's like to survive a Crisis, but they reap all the benefits of the stability won during that Crisis. They come of age as young adults during an Awakening with a desire to

---

[27] Strauss & Howe, 80-100.

reshape society into their idealistic view. Prophets under-protect their children in an effort to give them the social freedom they think everyone should have. Prophets are a dominant generation, independently shaping the attitudes of their era.

Nomad – Nomads are a reactive generation and are recessive, not dominant. They rely on others to help shape their attitudes and bring them an identity. They are the under-protected children of an Awakening and come of age during a time of Unraveling. During an Unraveling society looks for strong young adult leaders, and the Nomads are unable to fill that role. However, Nomads emerge as reluctant middle-aged leaders during the next Crisis.

Hero – Heroes are a civic generation. They are also a dominant generation that takes charge during the time of Crisis. They tear down failing institutions and rebuild them for the next High. They were born after an Awakening, are children of the Unraveling, and come of age during the Crisis to become the heroes of it. While doing their civic duty, they increasingly protect their children from the Crisis. They enjoy the High as mid-lifers and are strong, powerful elders during the next Awakening.

Artists – Artists are an adaptive generation. Born during the time of Crisis, they grew up overprotected by preoccupied Heroes. They come of age during the High and become midlife leaders of an Awakening. The majority of their adult life is characterized by institutional stability, and they are the beneficiaries of that stability. They have the freedom and ability to be and do almost anything they want.

HOW THE GENERATIONS FIT THIS MODEL

To see this cycle at work, let's take a look at the generations already discussed in this book. We'll also add to them additional older generations so that each archetype and turning is represented twice.[28]

The Missionary Generation (b. 1860–1882) was a Prophet generation. Born at the end of a Crisis turning, the American Civil War, they grew up during a High turning, which was reconstruction and the Gilded Age. Rapid economic growth and the Second Industrial Revolution characterized this High. Young adulthood saw them transition to a time of Awakening, which was characterized by a series of great spiritual revivals, specifically the Third Great Awakening. A sense of missionary urgency arose in the world. New religious groups, such as the Holiness movement, Seventh Day Adventists, and Christian Science, emerged.[29] The

---

[28] Strauss & Howe, 134-137.

[29] Justo L Gonzalez, *The Reformation to the Present Day*, vol. 2 of *The Story of Christianity: The Early Church to the Present Day* (Peabody: Prince Press, 1999), 253-261, 306-308.

Missionary Generation became a dominant generation that demanded greater social and religious accountability.

The Lost Generation (b. 1883–1900) was a Nomad generation. They were children of the Awakening led by the Missionary Generation. As institutions were attacked and social and spiritual freedom were championed, the Lost Generation grew up to be young adults of an Unraveling. This Unraveling led them to involvement in low social morality, speakeasies, prohibition, and gangster culture, all of which contributed to the naming of their generation. Further unraveling can be seen in World War I, where the entire world felt the effects of this era. The Lost Generation became a recessive generation, defined as "lost" by their parent generation, never fully developing their own unique dominant identity. A great representation of this generation is F. Scott Fitzgerald's *The Great Gatsby*.[30]

The GI Generation (b. 1901–1927) was a Hero generation. They were born and raised during the time of the Unraveling of the Lost Generation. The GI Generation came of age during a time of extreme Crisis with the Great Depression and World War II. The efforts of this generation to tear down the corrupt institutions of

---

[30] F Scott Fitzgerald, *The Great Gatsby* (New York: Scribner, 2004); "The Great Gatsby," IMDB, http://www.imdb.com/title/tt1343092 (accessed April 14, 2016).

the world and to rebuild financial and social stability saved not only the United States but also the world. What they did during the Crisis built the next High, in which they were middle-aged leaders at the start of the next first turning in the cycle. They became a dominant generation that shaped the world into a better place.

The Silent Generation (b. 1928–1945) are an Artist generation with the major characteristic of Stability. They were born in the midst of world crisis and came of age during the height of the American Superpower, the most recent High era. This era was characterized by a scientific and technological revolution. Silents have had the freedom and social stability to become and do whatever they wanted with nearly 100% job fulfillment. In middle age, they saw the next Awakening era, as their children demanded social justice against the tyranny of governmental institutions, especially in the light of the Vietnam War. The younger Silent Generation began fighting for creative, intellectual, and social freedoms as seen in Desegregation, Civil Rights movements, Women's Liberation movements, and Anti–War movements. They became a recessive generation, largely defined by the success of their parents and the demands of their children.

The Baby Boomer Generation (b. 1946–1964) are a Prophet generation with the major characteristic of Control. They were born during the High turning of the

American Superpower and became adults at the dawn of the Awakening of the Consciousness Revolution. They sought their own path and demanded their own unique identity not defined by institutionalism or by their parents. They rode the wave of the High and the Awakening to be free spirits and then middle-aged leaders during the next Unraveling turning. This Unraveling saw the Culture Wars of the 80s and the development of Postmodernism, where individualism was at its highest and institutions were weakest. Now they are becoming strong elders during the current Crisis era.

Generation X (b. 1965–1982) are a Nomad generation with the major characteristics of Respect. They are recessive to their dominant Baby Boomer parents. They were born in the Awakening and were under-protected as children by their free-spirit parents. They became young adults during the Unraveling of the Culture Wars and Postmodernism, the recession of the 80s, and the collapse of the Superpower era in the world. Like their equivalent the Lost Generation, they were defined as "lost" or "worthless" by their parent generation, and never fully developed a unique dominant identity. Middle-age has brought them into the current Crisis era as reluctant and somewhat unconfident leaders.

The Millennial Generation (b. 1983–2000) are our current Hero generation with the major characteristic of

Inclusion. They will dominate social development, tear down failing institutions, and rebuild them in the midst of the current historical turning, a Crisis era. Events that have defined our current Crisis era have been the 2008 economic recession and the War on Terror. Like the previous Hero generation, the GI Generation, Millennials are the ones fighting this war and will be the ones to rebuild the economy in its wake. They were children of the Unraveling at the end of the 20th century and have come of age during the current Crisis. They will be middle age leaders of the next first turning, the next High, and will be elders during the next Awakening.

The iGeneration (b. 2001–*2020?*) is our next Artist generation. They are children of the current Crisis and will come of age in the next High turning. Like the previous Artist generation, the Silent generation, they are most likely going to enjoy a time of economic and social stability and peace which will be built for them by the Millennial generation. They will have greater creative freedom and job opportunities and will enjoy a society ripe for their children, the next Prophet generation.

According to the Generational Cycle theory, Millennials and the GI Generation share common characteristics, such as social engagement and confidence. The historical events that shaped these generations are similar even if their specific generational personalities might differ. The Missionary Generation and Boomers also share characteristics, specifically a sense of self-sufficiency and a desire to shape their own destiny. It's perhaps easier to see how the Gen Xers and the Lost Generation share characteristics, both being generations lamented by society for their faults. The iGeneration, though still young and developing, will most likely take on personalities similar to that of the Silent Generation.

REFLECTION QUESTIONS

1. Is your generation an Artist, Prophet, Nomad, or Hero generation?

2. How is your generation reacting to the current historical turning?

3. Based on your generational archetype, what can you do to help influence the other generations?

4. What can you do to help influence the next historical turning?

CHAPTER 10

THE CYCLE OF THE CHURCH

"According to the grace of God which was given to me, like a wise master builder I laid a foundation, and another is building on it. But each man must be careful how he builds on it. For no man can lay a foundation other than the one which is laid, which is Jesus Christ." 1 Corinthians 2:10-11

If we apply this Generational Cycle to the church, there are some interesting finds that might help the modern church plan for the future. Like history and like generational characteristics, the church also has a corresponding cycle. Each generation has played a role in building the church throughout history. So as we seek to understand the generations within the church, it may also help to understand how those generations are affecting the future development of the church. To do that, we must look closer at how the historical cycle of the church has unfolded.

Awakening Eras and the Church

TURNING	HISTORICAL TREND	HISTORICAL EVENTS	CHURCH TREND	CHURCH EVENT
Awakening 1517–1542	Institutions attacked/ Individualism championed	Protestant Reformation	Revival	Protestant Reformation
Awakening 1621–1649	Institutions attacked/ Individualism championed	Puritan Revolution	Revival	Puritan Revolution
Awakening 1727–1746	Institutions attacked/ Individualism championed	First Great Awakening	Revival	First Great Awakening
Awakening 1822–1844	Institutions attacked/ Individualism championed	Second Great Awakening	Revival	Second Great Awakening
Awakening 1886–1908	Institutions attacked/ Individualism championed	Third Great Awakening	Revival	Third Great Awakening
Awakening 1964–1984	Institutions attacked/ Individualism championed	Consciousness Revolution/ Vietnam	Revival	Jesus Movement

Awakening eras have seen revivals in the church. As far back as the Protestant Reformation, each Awakening era has had a significant revival movement. The Protestant Reformation, the Puritan Revolution, the First Great Awakening, and the Second Great Awakening all happened with each turning of the Awakening era. Our most recent Awakening eras were no different. At the end of the 1800s, there was the Third Great Awakening; and in the 1960s and 70s, we had the Jesus Movement. The Prophet Generation were mostly children or teens during these times and the Artist Generation were young to middle adults. Artists and Hero generations led these times of revival.

In the most recent revival movement it was the GI Generation and the Silent Generation who led. Baby Boomers were children and teenagers at the beginning of this turning, and Gen Xers were children near the end.

Unraveling Eras and the Church

TURNING	HISTORICAL TREND	HISTORICAL EVENTS	CHURCH TREND	CHURCH EVENT
Unraveling 1542–1569	Weak Institutions/ Strong Individuals	Intolerance & Martyrdom	Fundamentalism	Counter–Reformation/ Council of Trent
Unraveling 1649–1675	Weak Institutions/ Strong Individuals	Colonial Unrest	Fundamentalism	Clarendon Code
Unraveling 1746–1773	Weak Institutions/ Strong Individuals	French Indian War/ Deism & empiricism	Fundamentalism	Rationalist & Pietist Movements
Unraveling 1844–1860	Weak Institutions/ Strong Individuals	Mexican War/ Dred Scott/ Underground Railroad	Fundamentalism	Oxford Movement
Unraveling 1908–1929	Weak Institutions/ Strong Individuals	WWI & Prohibition	Fundamentalism	American Fundamentalism
Unraveling 1984–2001	Weak Institutions/ Strong Individuals	National Debt/ Culture Wars	Fundamentalism	Conservative Resurgence

Immediately following the revivals of the Awakening eras, Unraveling eras saw a division in religious thought. There was an initial increase in religious liberalism, whether true liberalism or merely the perception of liberalism, followed immediately by a surge in fundamentalism.

After the Protestant Reformation, there came the Counter–Reformation and the Council of Trent to reestablish traditional Catholic doctrine. After the Puritan Revolution, a series of legislations called the Clarendon Code restored the Church of England and its dominance, especially in the enforcement of the 1662 Act of Uniformity.

After the First Great Awakening, there was a rise of intellectual deism and empiricism, which drew the critiques of David Hume. Meanwhile, the Rationalists and the Pietist movements both attacked intellectual and religious dogmatism from different angles. After the Second Great Awakening, while the United States was spiraling out of control toward the American Civil War, fundamentalism could be seen in the Oxford Movement in Europe.

The Third Great Awakening was followed by American Fundamentalism in the 1910s and 20s, and most recently the Jesus Movement was followed by the Conservative Resurgence in the Southern Baptist Convention, the largest protestant denomination in the United States.

During these surges of fundamentalism in the church, the Nomad Generation were mostly the children and teenagers, and the Prophet Generations were the young to middle adults. Prophets and Artists mostly led these movements.

Specifically, during the most recent fundamentalist movement, the Silent Generation and Baby Boomers were the most influential leaders. Gen Xers were children and teenagers at the beginning of this turning, and Millennials were children near the end.

Crisis Eras and the Church

TURNING	HISTORICAL TREND	HISTORICAL EVENTS	CHURCH TREND	CHURCH EVENT
Crisis 1569–1594	Social and Cultural Crisis/ Institutions torn down and rebuilt	Spanish/English Conflict	Division and Creativity	Protestant settlements/ Religious Flight
Crisis 1675–1704	Social and Cultural Crisis/ Institutions torn down and rebuilt	1st Indian War & English Revolution	Division and Creativity	Act of Toleration
Crisis 1773–1794	Social and Cultural Crisis/ Institutions torn down and rebuilt	American Revolution	Division and Creativity	Religious Freedom/ Circuit Riders/ Sunday Schools
Crisis 1860–1865	Social and Cultural Crisis/ Institutions torn down and rebuilt	American Civil War	Division and Creativity	Church Racism Propaganda
Crisis 1929–1946	Social and Cultural Crisis/ Institutions torn down and rebuilt	Great Depression & WWII	Division and Creativity	Faith Distinctions/ Radio Broadcast

| Crisis 2001– 2020? | Social and Cultural Crisis/ Institutions torn down and rebuilt | 2008 Recession & War on Terror | Division and Creativity | Progressive Christianity/ Relational Church/ Multisite/ Internet |

Crisis eras saw people seeking God for reasons beyond mere religion, effectively separating the devout from the apathetic, and creating increasingly distinct lines of religious thought. Toleration, division, financial struggles, and unique creative responses to maintaining church identity were typical during a Crisis.

After the Counter–Reformation, the Crisis was seen in the prolonged conflict between Spain and England. Increased political unrest and religious persecution at the hands of the fundamentalists brought a surge of religious flight to the New World. Here we clearly see division and creative response.

After the Clarendon Code, the Crisis era saw the First Indian War in the Americas in 1675 and Revolution in England in 1688. Implemented after the Revolution, the Act of Toleration required religious factions that dissented from the Church of England to register in order to have freedom of worship. It was a step toward tolerance, but also drew sharp dividing lines between groups of dissenting religious theological ideas. Here we clearly see toleration and division.

After the Rationalists and Pietist movements, the American Revolution defined the next Crisis era. During this time freedom of religion was secured in the Americas, but in England the Act of Toleration was extended to include Catholics with the Catholic Relief Act of 1791. Religious freedom throughout the world became increasingly strong but also more clearly defined into factions. Churches in the United States struggled financially to support their own ministers and had to use creative strategies in order to keep churches and Christians active; thus Circuit Riders were born. Here we see all the markers: toleration, division, financial struggles, and creative response.

Immediately after the fundamentalist Oxford Movement, the American Civil War defined the next Crisis era.[31] This era was abbreviated because the Civil war caused the absence of a Hero generation and an uncharacteristic jump in the pattern of turnings. During this short Crisis era, the church saw sharp divisions over slavery. Many pastors supported slavery while others preached against it. Religious tensions ran high with different opinions on what proper Biblical interpretation might be. Racism was just as divisive in religion as it was in the culture. Here we clearly see division, but we also see a push for racial toleration with creative responses on both sides and financial problems continuing through Reconstruction.

During the Great Depression and World War II, churches saw faiths deepen, even if church growth was slow. The lines between genuine Christians and genuine non-believers became clearer, with fewer people

---

[31] Straus & Howe, 121.

bothering to fake social religion. Churches turned to creative outreach through radio ministry as a way to increase their message. Here we see obvious financial problems and creative outreach strategies, as well as cultural religious division.

In our current Crisis era, we are seeing something very similar to the previous Crisis. Church attendance is declining, but the most recent research suggests that it is because those calling themselves Christians for social reasons are no longer doing so.[32] What is left in the church are genuine believers who are working hard to deepen their faith.

The previous Crisis era saw churches seeking creative strategies and restructuring in order to remain relevant, such as adopting new financial practices and broadcasting on the radio. Today, churches are seeking new creative strategies for the same reasons, once again needing to rethink financial practices and utilizing online broadcasting.

The Prophet generation mostly leads during these times, alongside elderly Artists, and they transition that leadership to the next Hero generation as they come of

---

[32] Kelly Shattuck, "7 Startling Facts: An Up Close Look at Church Attendance in America," Church Leaders, http://www.churchleaders.com/pastors/pastor-articles/139575-7-startling-facts-an-up-close-look-at-church-attendance-in-america.html (accessed April 14, 2016); Thom S. Rainer, "Seven Key Reasons Your Church Attendance May Be Declining," Thom S. Rainer, http://thomrainer.com/2015/07/seven-key-reasons-your-church-attendance-may-be-declining/ (accessed April 14, 2016).

age.

Nomads should be leaders during these Crisis eras; but because they came of age in an Unraveling, they usually are not. Usually they are skipped and leadership is retained by older generations and given to the next Hero generation as soon as they begin to come of age. If Nomads become Crisis leaders at all, it is with reluctance.

The Lost Generation (Nomads) were weak in religious leadership, with the two most notable being Karl Barth (1886) born at the beginning of the generation and A.W. Tozer (1897) born at the end. However, both were what was described earlier as break babies and may have identified with a different generation.

Today Gen Xers are the most missing generation in the church, and church leaders struggle to find ways to bring them back.[33] Baby Boomers and Gen Xers should be leaders together, but the Generational Would has made that almost impossible. Most of the church leadership has been retained by Baby Boomers and elderly Silents. Essentially skipping Gen Xers, Boomers are beginning to bring Millennials alongside them to train as their replacements.

---

[33] Adams, 41.

High Eras and the Church

TURNING	HISTORICAL TREND	HISTORICAL EVENTS	CHURCH TREND	CHURCH EVENT
High 1478–1517	Strong Institutions/ Weak Individuals	Tudor Renaissance	Church Growth and Stability	A new status quo of success.
High 1594–1621	Strong Institutions/ Weak Individuals	English Renaissance	Church Growth and Stability	A new status quo of success.
High 1704–1727	Strong Institutions/ Weak Individuals	British Superpower	Church Growth and Stability	A new status quo of success.
High 1794–1822	Strong Institutions/ Weak Individuals	American Independence/Romanticism	Church Growth and Stability	A new status quo of success.
High 1865–1886	Strong Institutions/ Weak Individuals	Reconstruction/ Gilded Age/ 2nd Industrial Revolution	Church Growth and Stability	A new status quo of success.
High 1946–1964	Strong Institutions/ Weak Individuals	American Superpower/ Desegregation	Church Growth and Stability	A new status quo of success.

Finally, High eras are characterized by church growth and stability. During our most recent High era, the 40s-60s, the church saw unprecedented growth. This growth came about by the steadfastness of the genuinely faithful and the innovation of church leaders to use cutting edge methods to bring the Gospel to a growing audience. But because of the rise of scientific intellectualism and the strength of institutions during the High, the church fell into an institutionalized pattern. Churches simply persisted in the programs already developed without much effort to continue innovation.

The two High eras ago saw growth and stability forced upon the church through direct intervention and institutionalization by the United States Government during post-American Civil War. The High preceding that was found during post-American Revolution independence. Obviously, freedom of religion was highly celebrated, and churches found new growth and stability.

Hero generations largely contributed to this growth and stability, which they passed on to the Artist generations to maintain.

With a surge in church growth built on the innovation being done now during this current Crisis, we can most likely expect a similar pattern when we reach the next High era. The Millennials (Heroes) will build a form of institutionalized stability in the church, which they will pass on to the iGeneration (Artists) to maintain. Following this, the Millennials as elders and iGen as midlifers will most likely lead some form of revival movement during the next Awakening era. A surge in fundamentalism, led by elder iGens and the next Prophet generation, will follow that in the future Unraveling era.

Perhaps the following comprehensive chart will make the patterns clearer.

All Historical Eras and the Church

TURNING	HISTORICAL TREND	HISTORICAL EVENTS	CHURCH TREND	CHURCH EVENT
High 1478–1517	Strong Institutions/ Weak Individuals	Tudor Renaissance	Church Growth and Stability	A new status quo of success.
Awakening 1517–1542	Institutions attacked/ Individualism championed	Protestant Reformation	Revival	Protestant Reformation
Unraveling 1542–1569	Weak Institutions/ Strong Individuals	Intolerance & Martyrdom	Fundamentalism	Counter–Reformation/ Council of Trent
Crisis 1569–1594	Social and Cultural Crisis/ Institutions torn down and rebuilt	Spanish/English Conflict	Division and Creativity	Protestant settlements/ Religious Flight
High 1594–1621	Strong Institutions/ Weak Individuals	English Renaissance	Church Growth and Stability	A new status quo of success.
Awakening 1621–1649	Institutions attacked/ Individualism championed	Puritan Revolution	Revival	Puritan Revolution
Unraveling 1649–1675	Weak Institutions/ Strong Individuals	Colonial Unrest	Fundamentalism	Clarendon Code
Crisis 1675–1704	Social and Cultural Crisis/ Institutions torn down and rebuilt	1st Indian War & English Revolution	Division and Creativity	Act of Toleration
High 1704–1727	Strong Institutions/ Weak Individuals	British Superpower	Church Growth and Stability	A new status quo of success.
Awakening 1727–1746	Institutions attacked/ Individualism championed	First Great Awakening	Revival	First Great Awakening

106 | We Are One

TURNING	HISTORICAL TREND	HISTORICAL EVENTS	CHURCH TREND	CHURCH EVENT
Unraveling 1746–1773	Weak Institutions/ Strong Individuals	French Indian War/ Deism & empiricism	Fundamentalism	Rationalist & Pietist Movements
Crisis 1773–1794	Social and Cultural Crisis/ Institutions torn down and rebuilt	American Revolution	Division and Creativity	Religious Freedom/ Circuit Riders/ Sunday Schools
High 1794–1822	Strong Institutions/ Weak Individuals	American Independence/Romanticism	Church Growth and Stability	A new status quo of success.
Awakening 1822–1844	Institutions attacked/ Individualism championed	Second Great Awakening	Revival	Second Great Awakening
Unraveling 1844–1860	Weak Institutions/ Strong Individuals	Mexican War/ Dred Scott/ Underground Railroad	Fundamentalism	Oxford Movement
Crisis 1860–1865	Social and Cultural Crisis/ Institutions torn down and rebuilt	American Civil War	Division and Creativity	Church Racism Propaganda
High 1865–1886	Strong Institutions/ Weak Individuals	Reconstruction/ Gilded Age/ 2nd Industrial Revolution	Church Growth and Stability	A new status quo of success.
Awakening 1886–1908	Institutions attacked/ Individualism championed	Third Great Awakening	Revival	Third Great Awakening
Unraveling 1908–1929	Weak Institutions/ Strong Individuals	WWI & Prohibition	Fundamentalism	American Fundamentalism
Crisis 1929–1946	Social and Cultural Crisis/ Institutions torn down and rebuilt	Great Depression & WWII	Division and Creativity	Faith Distinctions/ Radio Broadcast
High 1946–1964	Strong Institutions/ Weak Individuals	American Superpower/ Desegregation	Church Growth and Stability	A new status quo of success.

TURNING	HISTORICAL TREND	HISTORICAL EVENTS	CHURCH TREND	CHURCH EVENT
Awakening 1964–1984	Institutions attacked/ Individualism championed	Consciousness Revolution/ Vietnam	Revival	Jesus Movement
Unraveling 1984–2001	Weak Institutions/ Strong Individuals	National Debt/ Culture Wars	Fundamentalism	Conservative Resurgence
Crisis 2001–2020?	Social and Cultural Crisis/ Institutions torn down and rebuilt	2008 Recession & War on Terror	Division and Creativity	Progressive Christianity/ Relational Church/ Multisite/ Internet

REFLECTION QUESTIONS

1. For the Silent (Artist) generation: How did your generation contribute to the growth/stability of the last High (1946-1964) and the revival movement of the 60s-70s? The following Unraveling/Crisis? How can you help the Millennials (Hero) build church stability for the next High era?

2. For the Boomer (Prophet) generation: How did your generation contribute to the revival movement of the 60s-70s and the fundamentalist surge of the 80s-90s? The following Crisis? How can you help bring Gen Xers into leadership positions now?

3. For the Gen X (Nomad) generation: How did your generation contribute to the last Unraveling? What responsibility do Gen Xers have in the current church Crisis? How can you get involved and contribute to church health?

4. For the Millennial (Hero) generation: How did your generation contribute to the current church Crisis? How can you work with other generations to build the next High era of the church? What legacy do you want to leave for the iGeneration?

CHAPTER 11
MINISTRY STRATEGIES

"But the wisdom from above is first pure, then peaceable, gentle, reasonable, full of mercy and good fruits, unwavering, without hypocrisy. And the seed whose fruit is righteousness is sown in peace by those who make peace." James 3:17-18

It's easy to take this information and keep it external, thinking that others must change and adapt according to what has been said. Yet there is value here for everyone, even if some of the generational characteristics missed the mark on you as an individual.

Here are some ministry strategies that can be practically applied to the daily workings of the church. There are some general strategies that summarize what has been said about each individual generation and are meant to be the bigger picture that can help leadership have a snapshot of what's going on in the church demographic. But perhaps the most helpful for you, reader, are the sections that are *to* and *for* each generation.

I've taken the information in this book and I've used

it to generate specific ministry strategies *for* each generation. These are things the other generations need to be mindful of if they're going to create an effective ministry for that age group. I've also taken the information and compiled it *to* each generation, speaking directly to them and being real about their weaknesses and strengths to challenge them to a greater form of unity with other generations.

Keep in mind, however, that people are incredibly complex. Knowing how they might interact with each other does not mean those interactions can be controlled. Though I've written the book on generational interactions in the church and I can reasonably predict what will happen when these generations interact, often I feel powerless to prevent the inevitable conflict.

These strategies will work best when all parties involved have studied this information and have made a conscious decision to be a unifying church member that actively seeks to bridge generational conflict.

GENERAL STRATEGIES

The Silent Generation

Silents prefer generational inclusiveness, not generational specific ministry. They believe unity is best seen when the entire church is together. As a result, they enjoy corporate gatherings more than small groups, and they enjoy seeing the younger generations join them in these large settings.

Silents work well in administrative roles, and as this generation ages, they will need opportunities to continue to nurture and help the church to the best of their ability. They will need help keeping their environment from changing too fast when they are no longer able to care for themselves or help the church.

Often Silents recognize the need for church change, though they have trouble accepting it. Remember, stability in their environment is directly tied to their identity, and when they lose stability they feel as if like they are losing their identity. Church change should not come at the expense of their stability; rather they should be given some form of environment that is largely free from the changing church climate. Keep some active form of traditional programming, if only for this age group, even if it's not the major vision of the church.

Church change should not come at the expense of their stability.

When talking about spiritual matters, emphasis needs to be made on the stability and sufficiency of God and the Gospel of Jesus Christ to meet every need.

Millennials especially should learn to value the ideas of Silents. There's much to be learned from a generation that grew up in a Christian society similar to the one we keep saying we want, even if the methods to reach culture have changed.

Silents are the elder Artist generation, and our current Crisis era is likely to be the last historical era they experience fully. They feel the weight of the Crisis more than you think, and this threatens their stability in a huge way. They came of age during the previous High and long to experience that kind of church stability again. Help them to focus on the stability of God instead.

The Baby Boomer Generation

Boomers are inner-focused masters of their own destiny, and this can also apply to their spiritual life and church involvement. Boomers need a task to control. Giving them areas of continued responsibility, even after they have transitioned out of leadership, helps them to continue to feel useful in the church.

Boomers need to begin training their replacements.

Boomers need to be encouraged to train their replacements. When change comes to the church, Boomers need to see the benefit to their personal fulfillment and need to be given opportunities to help bring about the change.

When talking about spiritual matters, Boomers need to be reminded that God is in control of their lives, not them; but they also need to be reminded that their spiritual life with God is their responsibility, thereby placing some measure of control back into their hands. They are seekers of truth and spiritual revelation as it affects them directly, and Boomers want to hear the deeper mysteries found in the Bible explained clearly.

Xers should be middle-aged leaders during our current Crisis era, but they are missing. Xers should learn to recognize Boomer criticism as concern rather than hostility.

Boomers have had to fill the gap in many cases, but in some cases, Boomers are just reluctant to give up the control. Boomers will work together with Millennials to help shape our next High era. Help them to understand that no matter how frustrating it gets right now, God is ultimately in control.

Generation X

The Postmodern mindset makes Xers open to apologetic evangelism. They don't want to just know what they are supposed to believe but why they are supposed to believe it. They want to know they are respected, loved, and important to the church.

Low-hype, high-tech multimedia and creative strategies that emphasize fellowship, relationship, and family values will be the most attractive to them. Churches that are successful in attracting Gen Xers use highly informal, contemporary, and seeker-friendly strategies. Also, a church that seeks and promotes inclusivity rather than exclusivity is more likely to attract them.

Boomers especially should make a conscious effort to

encourage and respect Xers and to bite their tongues if necessary to keep from correcting them. If Xers feel criticized, disrespected, or feel as if they are failing at a task, they will not only quit the task unfinished but may leave the church completely.

Xers may be more responsive to community outreach and small groups rather than in-church programming because so much damage was done in the minds of many Xers by hypocritical religious church members.

> *Work hard to value Xers who ARE involved in church.*

Xers are cautious about getting involved in anything that involves "church." As children, they were constantly invited to "church," encouraged to get involved in "church," and often forced to attend "church," but many were never discipled into a true relationship with God. It may be necessary to reach this generation by taking the institution of "church" out of the conversation completely and talk to them only about their relationship with God. As they grow with God and are discipled as Christians, then you may begin trying to get them involved with the larger fellowship.

Xers should be our major leaders in the church right now during this Crisis, but history paints the Nomad generation as a generation of reluctant leaders. Do not give up on them, but do not expect Xers to ever become a major influencing generation in the church. Work hard to value the ones that are.

The Millennial Generation

Millennials want solid answers to tough questions. They want the church to be genuine, to be concerned with the world, and to stop excluding people for any reason. Millennials are not impressed by superficial attempts to become more hip or attractive. They want more substance underneath.

When presenting the Gospel to a Millennial, use language that emphasizes the inclusion aspect of the Gospel: that Jesus died for all and that Jesus loves all. Avoid spending too much time on the condemnation for sin. Do not be theologically weak with them, just approach theology from the direction of inclusion.

Embrace Millennial ideas and give them room to flourish.

If a Millennial asks a question, be prepared to give an honest answer with Scriptural support. If the question is too difficult, work with them to find the answer.

Millennials within the church are more likely to get involved in social and community outreach that brings healing and unity to hurting people around them, not just within the church walls.

Silents especially should make a conscious effort to

allow Millennials to approach church differently than they do without standing in the way.

Millennials are our current Hero generation, a generation that emerges from a Crisis era as strong leaders. During this Crisis time, they are finding their place and their voice in churches and will emerge during the next High as champions of church stability and growth. Embrace their ideas and give them room to flourish.

WHAT THIS MEANS

For the Silent Generation – We need to maintain a stable environment that respects the traditional forms of doing church, as well as other ministries in which Silents are involved in and view as important to the church. We need to hold on to and promote traditional elements that are relevant and supported by Scripture. Do not change for the sake of change. Changes should be predictable, slow, and with purpose.

To the Silent Generation – Recognize that some change DOES need to come because of the changing mindset of younger generations and the post-modern worldview dominant today. Allow traditions that are not Biblical or relevant to fade away and loosen emotional attachments to the physical things of the church. Work hard at understanding the Millennial Generation and understanding their worldview. Admit that doing ministry in this worldview is drastically different than the ministry techniques you grew up experiencing. Millennials are the church's future leaders, and if the church doesn't prepare for their leadership by adopting modern ministry methods, then there may be no future for your church.

For the Boomer Generation – Generate deep Bible studies that go beyond surface level teaching. Give Boomers tasks to control within the church. Allow Boomers to be intimately involved in church change, to help dictate how that change will come about, and to exercise in part some control in bringing it about.

To the Boomer Generation – Though you have a built-in drive to take charge, recognize that many of you are becoming too old to do everything. Serve as long as God leads you, but become mentors NOW to train your replacements. Seek out Gen Xers with love and respect, making all effort to heal the generational wound. When a Gen Xer does get involved, take a deep breath and step backward, being extra careful to build them up and not to criticize. Those "reluctant leaders" may surprise you if you give them the chance.

For the Gen Xers – Keep technology updated. Keep music programs dynamic and exciting. Build church groups and studies outside the building; program community and fellowship events beyond basic church activities; and use apologetic curriculum. In other words, emphasis should be made on the truth of the Bible and a genuine relationship with God over and above church rituals and tradition. Show them respect, but also show them you respect others in the love of Christ. Do not over-hype or try to over-sell church activities; be genuine and honest. Many Xers left because of hypocrisy and other harms done to them by "church," so Gen Xers are more likely to be reached when you take "church" things out of the equation and focus primarily on God. Don't be discouraged if you fail. Remember, Gen Xers are the most missing generation in the church and the most difficult to reach.

To the Gen Xers – Stop waiting and get involved. Stop playing the victim and giving excuses. Recognize that your center of self-worth comes from God, not from the opinions of others. Work to forgive Boomers for the generational wound and to step up alongside them in the church. Work to forgive religious hypocrisy and other harms done in the name of "church" and know that those things are not a reflection of genuine Christianity. Be willing to accept tradition when it is relevant rather than insisting on throwing the whole thing out. Accept *blended* worship that incorporates a wide range of worship styles instead of insisting on an all contemporary approach. Don't push change unless there is a well thought-out, legitimate reason. Even then don't push for quick change. Prove you can actually be the leader God created you to be.

For the Millennials – Be a church that is transparent and genuine. Love and acceptance should come from the entire church body, not just the staff. Show a concern for the community and a willingness to go to the sinners rather than have them come to the church. Deal with inclusive issues within the church, such as racism and social elitism, and work to build a worship environment that is inclusive to everyone and does not exclude anyone for any reason. Be prepared to give honest answers to tough life questions without regurgitating standard religious answers. Millennials with children will need quality Biblical education with consistent activity planning for their children. Make technology so integrated into the church environment that it is almost forgotten.

To the Millennials – You must work to understand the value of tradition and the faith heritage built by the previous generations, especially the Silent Generation. Things may not have always been good, and your church still exists because of their hard work. They also remember the church as it was during the last High era.

Respect that. Become a part of it, do not fight it. As emerging leaders, seek to evolve the church from within existing structures, not to throw everything out and start over. Change is needed and change will come but know that change takes time. Do not be overly impatient.

Recognize the inclusion problems in the church are a relic of an older culture and that older generations struggle to adopt new cultural ideas different than those they grew up with. It is not necessarily a symptom of the church itself. Work to build better inclusion by changing culture in and outside the church through an emphasis on scripture, not by attacking Christian brothers and sisters raised in that culture. DO NOT compromise on sound theology for the sake of inclusion. This will be the key to the next High era of church stability and growth, and it all depends on how you handle things now.

GENERAL KEY POINTS TO REMEMBER

Here are a few key points that synthesize the strategies and generational characteristics that have been discussed.

Remain updated – Culture moves fast and the people even faster sometimes. If the church is still stuck in ministry methods designed thirty to fifty years ago, the upcoming generations may think them irrelevant. Keep technology updated, focus on cultural relevancy, be mindful of first appearances, and be educated about modern theological concerns.

Inclusion – Recognize that exclusion is not a part of the Bible. The culture around you knows this and has dealt with this, especially the younger generations. Exclusion is a non-Biblical cultural relic that is still only viewed as positive by some people in older generations. It's time the church became inclusive. I'm not talking about becoming liberal in theology or membership practices, but understanding that Jesus came for all people and it's not right for the church to discriminate who does and does not get to come hear the Gospel.

Genuineness – The church must be transparent, real, and genuine in everything. Be genuine in worship, instead of going through the motions. Demonstrate genuineness in faith rather than saying one thing and acting another. The culture is sensitive to hypocrisy and political correctness, so do not try to be anything other than what you really are.

Dynamic blended worship – Attempt to build environments that minister to a broad variety of generational expectations. Use hymns alongside praise songs. Don't be afraid to bring in alternative instrumentation, but don't forsake traditional instrumentation either.

Dual education program of traditional and small groups – The discipleship process should also be built to accommodate a variety of generational expectations. Continue with traditional Sunday School and do it well, if only for older generations. Also, build small groups outside the church, perhaps as a new direction for Sunday nights, in order to bring in younger generations. Do not neglect children in your discipleship plan.

Multi-layer curriculum and discipleship – Constantly evaluate the audience and change curriculum based on needs. Use advanced Bible study for Boomers and apologetic studies for Xers. Studies that address deep life questions work best for Millennials.

Allow programming to evolve – Do not be afraid to evaluate programs and activities for their effectiveness. What worked ten years ago may not work for today's culture. Constant evaluation and adjustment of programs for continued effectiveness are essential. The current Crisis era is one characterized by creative ministry strategies. Embrace that creativity and allow it to be fluid to find the right strategies that will bridge the church to the next High era.

Promote healing, understanding, and interaction between the generations – Boomers and Xers should work to heal the wound. Silents and Millennials should work to understand and respect each other. Be cautious of these interactions, and if a conflict arises, step away and defer to a mediator. Work to find ways of making the differences in the church a strength of the church.

Plan for the future – Make a plan for church change and work the plan. Recognize that church isn't what it used to be and will never return to the old methods. The next eras of the church will be a High of stability and growth, followed by an Awakening of revival. These two events will happen over the course of the next fifty years. Lay the foundations now and be ready.

REFLECTION QUESTIONS

1. How can your church better minister to the Silent generation?

2. How can your church better minister to the Baby Boomer generation?

3. How can your church better minister to Generation X?

4. How can your church better minister to Millennials?

CHAPTER 12

NOW WHAT?

"Therefore be careful how you walk, not as unwise men but as wise, making the most of your time, because the days are evil. So then do not be foolish, but understand what the will of the Lord is." Ephesians 5:15-17

I realize that parts of this study may read like last month's horoscope, but I'm guessing that as I described each generation your mind immediately recognized those characteristics in people you know. Every time I have presented this information, it is met with nods of agreement and an overwhelming sense that each generation was properly represented and described.

It may be difficult to synthesize this information into your church. Just knowing how the generations are different is not enough if there is not a willingness to do something about it.

As we look across the church landscape, you almost see two types of churches when it comes to generational demographics. There are churches mostly populated by

Silents and Boomers with even some GI Generation that are still with us. Then there are churches that are mostly populated by Xers, Millennials, and their children. It's not that either side wants to be divided; it's that they feel the other side is too far separated to reconcile.

Reconciliation may be difficult even if these two types of churches did want to become united again. There may not be enough willingness from older generation churches to act on the information presented in this book, and even if there is a willingness, there is no guarantee the younger generations will respond accordingly.

There is hope for generational unity…

On the other hand, churches populated by the younger generations may not want to give up the modern ministry style they've grown to love in favor of adopting a blended ministry style that meets some of the older generation's traditional needs.

If the historical cycle of the church tells us anything, it's that the younger generations are in the process of tearing down and rebuilding the institution of the church and that it is futile to fight that restructuring. The next historical turning will see a newly restructured but functional church built on the innovation and creativity being done today. It will usher in a time of church growth and stability. The question becomes whether or not established older generation churches will survive to see the next High era or will newly-created younger generation churches merely grow to take their places.

I, for one, still think there is hope for generational unity—otherwise, I wouldn't have written this book. I implore older generation and younger generation churches to take generational unity seriously. Generational unity is definitely God's will for the church, and this study is meant to give you some of the tools and information you'll need to foster that kind of unity. But it won't be easy. It takes commitment and patience on the part of everyone involved. Approach it with fervent prayer, and the rest may just come naturally as God leads you to work together.

We do not need to ignore the implications of internal conflict, especially when it can be avoided. There are many superficial implications…declining attendance, declining budgets, and the closing of established churches. But the collateral implications are far more urgent.

Consider the "missing." These are the epidemically high percentages of Gen Xers and Millennials who do not attend church at all. Though we don't know every case, there is a high chance that a non-church goer is also not a Christian. Isn't generational unity worth the mission of reaching the lost?

Also consider the reputation of the church. Our culture doesn't even know what a genuine Christian looks like. Our actions and our words show division, not unity. Shouldn't we represent the best of humanity to a lost culture?

As always, change begins with YOU. Each individual must make a commitment to be the best representation of Christ that they can possibly be.

We must first examine our own hearts and tend our own relationships with Christ. Do you want to be unified? Do you want to reach the lost? It starts here, dealing with those generational weaknesses we all carry but don't want to admit they exist. Prayer is the key. Real, genuine prayer...that seeks the face of God, is honest with the darkness still in our hearts, and is ready to do whatever it takes to further the kingdom of God. We cannot pray for change in our churches or our communities until we first learn to pray for change within ourselves.

A willingness to be unified must come from an individual desire to humble ourselves before others, to become less so that Christ will become more, and to let our common bond of love become the catalyst for our unity. And when the individuals of the church have found this kind of unifying humility before the cross, then the church is ready to be unified.

This is what the church is meant to be.

This is unity.

This is how we become one.

REFLECTION QUESTIONS

1. How can you be more generationally inclusive as an individual?

2. What things about yourself do you need to work on?

3. How can you contribute to a generationally unified plan for your church?

BIBLIOGRAPHY

Adams, Chris, ed. *Women Reaching Women.* 1997. Rev. ed. Nashville: Lifeway Press, 2005.

"America During WW II: Churches." Children In History. http://histclo.com/country/us/chron/940/ww2/home/ww2us-church.html (accessed April 13, 2016).

Barna, George. *Baby Busters: The Disillusioned Generation.* Chicago: Northfield Publishing, 1994.

———. *The Second Coming of the Church.* Nashville: Word Pub., 1998.

Carlson, Elwood. *The Lucky Few: Between the Greatest Generation and the Baby Boom.* Dordrecht: Springer, 2008.

Craig, Bill, and Donna Gandy. *Respect: Meaningful Ministry with Baby Boomers in Your Church and Community.* Nashville: Lifeway Press, 2009.

Epstein, Dan. *C20th Pop Culture.* North Vancouver, B.C.: Whitecap Books, 1999.

Gravett, Linda, and Robin Throckmorton. *Bridging the Generation Gap.* Franklin Lakes, NJ: Career Press, 2007.

Gonzalez, Justo L. *The Reformation to the Present Day.* Vol. 2 of *The Story of Christianity: The Early Church to the Present Day.* Peabody: Prince Press, 1999.

Newport, Frank. "Questions and Answers about Americas' Religion." Gallup. http://www.gallup.com/poll/103459/questions-answers-about-americans-religion.aspx (accessed April 13, 2016).

"Generation." Wikipedia, the Free Encyclopedia. https://en.wikipedia.org/wiki/Generation (accessed April 13, 2016).

Lancaster, Lynne C., and David Stillman. *When Generations Collide: Who They Are, Why They Clash, How to Solve the Generational Puzzle at Work.* New York: HarperCollins, 2002.

Rainer, Thom S. "Seven Key Reasons Your Church Attendance May Be Declining." Thom S. Rainer. http://thomrainer.com/2015/07/seven-key-reasons-your-church-attendance-may-be-declining/ (accessed April 14, 2016).

———. "The Buster Generations." *Leading Adults.* Winter 2003-2004, 26-27.

Rainer, Thom S., and Jess W. Rainer. *The Millennials: Connecting to America's Largest Generation.* Nashville, Tenn: B&H Pub. Group, 2011.

Shattuck, Kelly. "7 Startling Facts: An Up Close Look at Church Attendance in America," Church Leaders. http://www.churchleaders.com/pastors/pastor-articles/139575-7-startling-facts-an-up-close-look-at-church-attendance-in-america.html (accessed April 14, 2016).

Strauss, William, and Neil Howe. *The Fourth Turning: An American Prophecy*. New York: Broadway Books, 1998.

Stetzer, Ed, and Mike Dodson. *Comeback Churches: How 300 Churches Turned Around and Yours Can Too*. Nashville, Tenn.: B & H Pub. Group, 2007.

Underwood, Chuck. *The Generational Imperative: Understanding Generational Differences in the Workplace, Marketplace and Living Room*. North Charleston, SC: BookSurge, 2007.

Veith, Gene Edward. *Postmodern Times: A Christian Guide to Contemporary Thought and Culture*. Turning Point Christian Worldview Series. Wheaton, Ill.: Crossway Books, 1994.

"W.W. II Brought Americans Back to Church." Old Magazine Articles. http://www.oldmagazinearticles.com/WW2-church-attendance-American-church-attendance-increased-during-world-war-two#.Vul_lkfuMY8 (accessed April 13, 2016)

Made in the USA
San Bernardino, CA
03 August 2018